# It's
## No Big Deal
### Really

# It's
# No Big Deal
# Really

## a parent's guide to making divorce easy for children

### anne cantelo

*f*

First published in 2007
by Fusion Press, a division of Satin Publications Ltd
101 Southwark Street
London SE1 0JF
UK
info@visionpaperbacks.co.uk
www.visionpaperbacks.co.uk
Publisher: Sheena Dewan

A catalogue record for this book is available from the British Library.

ISBN: 978-1-905745-24-1

2 4 6 8 10 9 7 5 3 1

Cover photo: Nishan Akgulian/Getty Images
Cover and text design by ok?design
Printed and bound in the UK by
Creative Print and Design (Wales), Ebbw Vale

*To my two daughters, Stephanie and Gabriella, who have been brave enough to encourage me to write this and to all the people who shared their experiences with me so candidly.*

# CONTENTS

# Introduction

I'm not a psychologist or a lawyer (although people from these professions did help me with my research); this book is about my experiences and the experiences of others that taught me so much about divorce and how it can affect children. I've written it in the hope that it will help others think through the issues and so avoid some of the worst mistakes. Unlike so many books on this subject, my experiences are not depressing; things can work out really well.

My own story is that my partner and I separated in 2001 and divorced in 2003. At the time of the separation my two daughters were aged 10 and 13 years old. I was very worried what this would mean to them; like most parents, their happiness means everything to me. But on top of that I believe that parents have an obligation to raise their children so that they benefit society and don't cause it problems. Divorce and single parents are held responsible for so many of society's ills that it was a very real concern to me. Our children are more likely to get into alcohol and drugs, to commit crime, to become parents prematurely and to perform badly at school.

I therefore hunted hard, but without success, for a book that would help ensure that my children were affected as little as possible. I found nothing suitable and instead was shocked by how much of the advice focused on the problems themselves, rather than suggestions on how to avoid them. These books suggested that the issues that divorce creates are unavoidable and consequently they made me even more depressed and feel more guilty. The rest looked at how to 'win' as much as you could from your ex in terms of money and access to your children; rather than winning the happy solution I wanted for them. The advice I received from others was similarly focused on the battle they said lay in front of me. I walked out of a lawyer's office when he warned me that I was entering a war and the best way to 'win' it was to start the attack. I was told on numerous occasions that I was naïve to think that I could avoid the divorce getting dirty and that it was not possible to have an amicable divorce. I'm happy to report that they were wrong.

It was the experiences of other people that I found most useful in giving me an insight into the long-term impact of typical behaviour during a divorce. I looked at evidence from psychologists and spoke to as many people as possible from all sides, children of divorce as well as parents. In effect this book gathers those anecdotes and research together and supplements it with new research. I've included both the mistakes and the things we got right, often by lucky accident.

Two years ago my younger daughter, Gabriella, then aged 14 years old, came home from school and told me that she'd spent the whole of her lunch hour comforting a friend whose parents had announced that they were getting divorced. I asked Gabriella what she'd told her friend. Gabriella shrugged in response, 'That it's no big deal really; you get to have two bedrooms, two holidays and a break from whichever parent is giving you hassle.' I was astonished and began to think again about how we'd reached that happy outcome (after, of course, challenging her view that I ever gave her 'hassle'!). Ultimately her comment led to me writing this book.

I'm pretty sure that Gabriella hasn't felt like that every step of the way; I've made loads of mistakes, I've been depressed and bad tempered and I'm sure my ex has had similar ups and downs. I know there were times when it must have felt like Gabriella's world was caving in. But to have reached the point where she can honestly say what she did proved the pessimists wrong. Divorce does not have to ruin your children's lives.

Some of the advice in this book is likely to irritate you. You might even throw the book across the room in disgust a few times. One revelation that I found fascinating is that if you accuse someone of something that they're confident is completely untrue it doesn't affect them emotionally; they won't get angry and probably won't even bother to argue. But if you tell someone something that they're worried may be true, then they'll argue it to prove to themselves, as much as the accuser, that they're in the right and they'll become quite emotional about it. Shakespeare clearly worked that one out a little ahead of me with, 'The lady doth protest too much, methinks.' It's a really useful insight when you're going through a divorce: if your husband or wife has some issues he or she gets unreasonably angry about he or she's probably feeling guilty.

It will also help you understand and use your own reactions to what I say in this book. If you find yourself getting angry with what I say then examine the cause carefully. What don't you want to be true? What evidence do you have that it's not true in your case? Can you be sure that the evidence is sound or should you check it out with someone impartial? I can only tell you what I discovered through my own experiences and the experiences of the people I spoke to. All children are different and all situations are different so I wouldn't want anyone to slavishly follow what I say to the letter; you know your children and your situation best, all I can do is to give you the benefit of hindsight in order to make sure you ask yourself the right questions. I've also tried to make it easier for you to look ahead to the long-term implications of the actions you're taking now. Many of the people I spoke to bitterly regret things they did that seemed fairly innocuous at the time but in hindsight were plain stupid (their words) and had a devastating long-term impact.

I know that not everyone will have such a mature and responsible ex as I did. I have him and his new wife to thank for helping our children get through this so well. Nor do I underestimate the potential problems caused by divorce and all the issues that surround it. I've heard some real horror stories so this book looks at how to manage them. Ultimately you can only ever be responsible for yourself, and good behaviour will eventually shame most people into being less of a pain. Similarly we are all unreasonable at least some of the time but fortunately apologising is as infectious as the common cold.

Many of the issues that affect marriages, such as adultery, mental illness and physical abuse, are major subjects by themselves that could easily take up the whole of this book if covered in any depth. However, as I've set out to give a general guide, and as these issues don't affect everyone, I've included headline advice only, so that you can investigate those areas that concern you further and so that it's clear where my more general advice doesn't apply.

Laws on divorce and financial issues vary from country to country and small differences in circumstances can also make huge differences to how the law will be applied. I've consequently only given an indication of what the law is likely to say and instead focused on the moral judgements you need to make and the implications these will have for your children. You should check how the law applies where you live and in your peculiar circumstances. You can find out the details of the law from your court or online, and information on the financial implications of your divorce on such things as pensions and mortgages from your financial advisor.

I've dealt with the issues roughly in chronological order, although it made sense for some issues to be grouped together rather than to follow this structure too strictly. And of course different circumstances mean that the order that things happen to you and your family may be different from the order suggested here.

Part-way through you'll think I'm asking you to make a lot of sacrifices for your children, but ultimately you'll find you benefit as much as they do; and not just because you'll have much happier children. There is an assumption that ensuring that your children are happy means always putting them first and sacrificing the needs of the adults concerned but I've found that to be untrue. If you ignore the needs of the adults you can increase the distress of the children.

My daughters are now young women who have great relationships with both their parents, have performed well at school and seem to have escaped most of the problems associated with teens. It is sorely tempting fate to write that and if between now and publication they become gangland criminals, alcoholics or junkies I might want to write a revision (but probably won't have time if I'm dealing with that lot).

I'm particularly grateful to the professional advice of Gill Jardine (BA HND Integrative Counselling, PGCE Advanced Certificate in Counselling Children and Young People, BACP Accreditation). She works with children who are going through their parents' divorce, so sees the issues you're now facing every day. I'm also grateful to all those who so candidly gave me the benefit of their experiences to include, particularly those whose experiences still give them pain to recall. Many of these contributors, parents, step-parents and children, cried on my shoulder; I sincerely hope that setting down these experiences in this way will help them to move on as much as it helps you to avoid that sort of pain. These people all shared my passion for improving the experience of other children by sharing their own successes and failures in the hope that we can all learn from them. In the interests of the children concerned their names, the names of parents and some minor details have been changed to maintain their anonymity.

I hope you decide you don't need to read beyond the first chapter, but if you do, then the aim of this book is to help you and your family find happiness again.

# CHAPTER 1

---

## DIVORCE OR STAY TOGETHER
## FOR THE SAKE OF THE CHILDREN

---

- What do your children want?
- Help to use and help to avoid
- Why do you want a divorce?
- The problems
- The crisis points
- The effect of children's age
- Expectations after the divorce
- To break or not to break

The popular view is that the divorce statistics are a sad indictment on modern-day society; I don't agree. Just like the invention of antibiotics, contraception, sanitation and pain-killers, I believe that the social acceptance of divorce has made our lives immeasurably better. I would have hated to have lived at a time when everyone had to stay married for life. Great if you chose well but terrible if you didn't. What is a sad indictment on modern-day society is the sexist and adversarial way that divorce is dealt with, which is usually the cause of the pain that children experience.

Some relationships work and some don't. It's part of life, and doesn't necessarily mean that either of the people concerned is at fault in some way. Until you become a parent the only people you really have to worry about are the two people involved. Once you and your partner produce children the rules of the game change; you'll never be out of each other's lives entirely, and that applies whether you're married or not. Many parents don't let this affect them and will happily produce children with different people without giving the break-ups any more thought than they did when they were childless; others will stick together 'for the sake of the children' however grim the marriage becomes. Neither approach is good for children.

I don't believe that the availability of divorce leads people to split up. It probably makes some people work less hard at their marriages than they would otherwise have had to, but most people realise that divorce actually takes a lot of guts, particularly when you have children. The easy option is to sit tight and live in a lifeless marriage. This suggests that in the past a very large percentage of people had to live in marriages that had broken down irretrievably (if today's statistics are any indication: as many as 50 per cent). Think what that meant: they were stuck with both the misery of living every day and every night with someone that they found irritating or didn't like and at the same time were denied that basic human need of loving and being loved. Think too how terrible it must have been for the children, who were raised in households that were filled with tension instead of love.

*Wendy's story:*

When my ex-husband used to come home my spirits sunk. I had to stay married longer than I wanted to because his father was ill. During that last year I became so depressed that I had a nervous breakdown and was off work for six months. My husband wasn't a bad person, but if we'd had to stay together I know I would have had to find another way out. I just couldn't stand it; I was so miserable.

In the past, marriages that had seemed doomed sometimes were revived. By having to stay together the couple found a way for their marriage to work again. Today many of those marriages would have resulted in divorce before they were given a chance to be saved. Is yours one of them? Before you separate you have a duty to your children, and to yourselves, to find out whether your marriage is salvageable. Is there a chance that you could be a happy family again?

# What do your children want?

Instead of assuming that staying together is best for the children you need to understand what your children's emotional needs are. I checked with a child counsellor and she advised that they can be divided into needs and desirables.

Needs for healthy emotional development:

- To feel safe and secure
- To feel valued and 'listened to'
- To have a home which is a sound base

- To have time to spend with peers (friends)
- To have some choice in how they use their free time
- To have access to age appropriate toys/surroundings

If they're very young (under five years old but sometimes older) they also need an 'attachment' figure.

Desirables for healthy emotional development:

- To have the love of both parents
- To have time with both parents
- To take part in activities which they enjoy and in which they can succeed

You may have other things to add to the lists for your children but think long term; look at the things your children will look back on. It will help if you think about your own childhood; what were the things that made it good or bad? What are your best memories and what are your worst? Your children may seem obsessed with material things but almost all these possessions will be in a landfill site in ten years' time, long forgotten. They'll remember experiences rather than things; their characters will be formed by the emotional support you give them as parents, the time they're able to spend with their friends and their triumphs both in school and outside. The triumphs can be quite small to make an impact on their self-esteem and be embedded in their memories for life.

My girls' paternal grandmother died when Gabriella was eight years old and we were speaking about her recently. Gabriella told me that she had only two memories of her. 'Sitting on her lap with her humming and when we were playing that game and no one could think of a drink beginning with the letter "n" except me. I was so pleased with myself.' So pleased that eight years on she still remembers it as one of her triumphs. (By the way, to stop your mind being diverted for the rest of this chapter, the answer is 'Nesquik'.)

Children are happiest when they have two loving parents to share their lives with them. Your children will probably desperately want you to stay together, but they may not be old enough to understand what that could mean. They will be terrified of the unknown and terrified that one of you will leave their lives for ever because of the divorce. Look again at your list. A bad marriage will not meet their need for a home that feels 'safe and secure'. Staying together, when you no longer love each other and feel irritated by each other, may mean condemning your children to growing up in a house full of tension. Conversely, if you handle the divorce sensitively you can still meet all their emotional needs and desires. The problems only come if you ignore one or more of your children's needs or desires, as people often do when they divorce.

### Pete's story:

My father was a very bad tempered, argumentative man. I was the youngest of five brothers and sisters and the whole house would go rigid with fear when he came home. His anger was normally directed at my mother; he even dragged her round by the hair a couple of times when he was unhappy with something and it was normally over trivial things. But he seemed to resent us too. I hated my childhood; I lived in constant fear and could never understand why my mother stayed. My earliest memories are hiding under the blankets and praying he would leave. He seemed to really hate my mother.

I left home as soon as I could; I didn't even go to university, just to get away from him. My parents separated and divorced soon after. I asked my mother why and she told me she'd stayed with him for the sake of us children. It was all I could do not to scream at her in frustration. It wasn't as if we would have been poor; she had a good job and we would have managed just fine.

I saw my father about a year after I left (I'd avoided him). He was a changed man, so much happier and more relaxed. He explained that the marriage had broken down so badly that it had got to the stage where he was irritated every time my mother entered the room. He'd found it incredibly difficult to live like that. He even apologised 'if' he'd been a bit bad tempered 'sometimes' but they had both agreed that they should not separate while the children were at home.

It's therefore your duty to look very seriously at the problems in your marriage and see if you can, in the near future, return it to a place that will give your children the support they need. Of course it won't happen overnight; it will need working on. Whether you stay married or divorce, keep referring to the list of emotional needs and desirables.

# Help to use and help to avoid

There is plenty of relationship support and professional guidance now available, such as relationship counsellors and mediators. Many have a fantastic record of retrieving happy marriages from ones heading for divorce. For the sake of your children you should therefore give it a try at least. At worst they will help you separate and divorce amicably.

Lawyers are there to give you legal advice, not marriage guidance: don't confuse the two. Asking a lawyer for advice on your relationship is like asking a confectioner to devise your diet plan. Using lawyers in the wrong way will cost you dearly, and not just financially (see Chapter 5).

Generally I would also avoid asking for help from friends and family. Family are most likely to side with their own or, in the case of parents and grandparents, be very keen to get you 'settled' again so that they can stop worrying about you. Friends, particularly mutual friends, may feel awkward at having to take sides, particularly if they are a couple who are friends with both of you. More significantly, their judgement will be based only on what you tell them, which is a bit like a jury only hearing the argument for the prosecution; and because the worse it sounds the more sympathy you'll get, you'll probably exaggerate a little – most people do. That also applies to online help in the form of chat rooms, etc. If you're careful about anonymity they can be useful places to download your anger but it's not possible for people in chat rooms to take a balanced view when they have only your side of things.

Being too honest about your problems with too many friends might also cause issues in the future. I think we've all been in the situation where we've been relieved at a friend breaking up with someone and said something we'd been dying to say along the lines of, 'I always thought he was a bastard and not to be trusted', and then had to make polite conversation with the 'bastard' when the couple made up, or even seen our friendship end because of our statement.

You will, however, need to have someone you can talk to openly, away from your spouse and the professionals. Try to limit this to one or two close friends. They will be there to help relieve the tension and offer a shoulder to cry on when you need it. You'll also find that it's often easier to come to decisions when you think out loud. You should choose friends who are clearly more yours than your partner's, and preferably not married to one of your spouse's friends. The best are those that don't go overboard on sympathy and advice but instead question and listen to you so that it is you making the judgements and decisions, not your friend. These friends should also be those that don't gossip. You want to be able to download your anger without it ever getting back to your children or your spouse. How do you know if someone is a gossip? Think back over your relationship with them. How many juicy bits of information have they given you about other people? Do they often start sentences with 'I shouldn't really tell you this, so you mustn't tell anyone else but I trust you and...' These friends are great sources of information but not to be trusted with keeping your private relationship issues private. If they tell you other people's secrets you can be sure that yours will soon be doing the rounds too. Things have a remarkable way of getting distorted to make a story juicier, and then being heard by the wrong ears. So pick your confidants very carefully and limit it to one or two.

## Why do you want a divorce?

You'll either have experienced a crisis in your marriage or you'll have a gradual realisation that you married the wrong person. Ultimately deciding whether or not you want a divorce is not about how your partner has behaved, but your reaction to it. Another person, in the same position as you, might continue in the marriage very happily. You therefore need to articulate your unhappiness to your spouse as early as possible and not assume that they know they're causing you problems. It's possible for one of you to be oblivious to how bad things have got until the crisis point is reached. However painful it is you need to make sure your spouse knows when they're behaving in a way that's making you consider ending the marriage in time to put it right.

## Karen's story:

We'd been married 12 years and had two children and I thought things were going fine. We had some arguments but no more than other people, I didn't think. I still loved Ian, my husband, a lot and he treated me in a way that suggested that he felt the same. In the last two years of our marriage we actually seemed to be arguing much less and when I had to go into hospital for a week he came to see me every day even though, with the children, that was really difficult for him. It was only a few weeks later that, during a pretty minor argument, he said he wanted us to separate. At first I was convinced there must be someone else, in many ways it would have been easier if there had been as I would have someone to blame. But there wasn't; he spent the next year living alone.

I found out later that he'd wanted to leave me for years but events kept happening that made him feel bad about it. He'd got to the point where he felt indifferent towards me, so couldn't even be bothered to argue, but he was so well brought up that he still felt the need to do 'his duty' by me, which explained why he visited me in hospital. I wish he'd told me earlier. He'd been making all these plans while it was just presented to me without any warning. I went from what I thought was a comfortable, happy marriage to being alone and unwanted.

# The problems

Almost all marriages will go through bad times. It's said that it takes 18 months to find out whether you really love someone enough to marry them. It probably takes a similar amount of time to decide whether your marriage is really unsalvageable.

In that time take a detached look at what the problems are and make an effort to rediscover what you loved about the person in the first place. Try to spend relaxed time alone with them. Give them constructive feedback on things that are affecting how you feel about them and try to do it in a calm, non-accusatory fashion. If possible, change things so that whatever it is that irritates you stops happening.

Sit down and list, for your eyes only, what you think the bugs are in your relationship. Be as honest as you can; even if some of the things on your list seem really trivial, if they affect you they're worth looking at. Your list will probably include variations and combinations of the following, most of them can be put right with a bit of work and lots of communication and commitment from both of you. Some are simpler than others.

## Boredom
Some marriages, particularly where people marry young, can get to a stage where your spouse is OK but things are very

boring. There's nothing terribly wrong with the marriage but you can't see yourself living like this for the rest of your life. You think you must be missing out on something. Is this really all there is to life?

It's possible to get these marriages working again, if you both put the effort in, and that usually means both inside and outside the bedroom. Essentially you need to pay more attention to each other. Many couples will sacrifice so much for their children that they leave nothing for themselves and their relationship. That's crazy when their relationship is key to the family being united and happy. Make sure you have some good babysitters and then don't feel guilty about doing things together where it's just about the two of you. Go out to dinner or to the cinema, go away for the weekend, go for walks through the woods and rediscover the people who've been buried under life's chores. If you still have itchy feet make sure you understand the realities of divorce (see below).

## You're doing more than your share of the chores

If both of you work you should do the same amount of household chores. By 'work' I include staying at home to care for the children. If you've grown resentful over how little you can get your partner to contribute the simple solution is to employ someone to clean for you; it may sound extravagant but it's a lot cheaper than divorcing over it. It helps to understand that there are two reasons behind the problem. The first is that many people still believe that housework is someone else's job (teenagers and many men are the worst culprits of this attitude). But the second reason, which is much more difficult to solve, is that each one of us can put up with a different level of dirt and mess before we feel uncomfortable living with it. With some people it's when a magazine or cushion is slightly askew, while at the other end of the scale some people don't feel uncomfortable with the dirt until the rats have moved in. If two people with widely divergent tolerances for cleanliness live together the person who needs their home clean and tidy will always capitulate long before the more laid-back partner recognises that anything needs to be done, which means that one person will always do a disproportionate amount of the housework. Nagging doesn't solve that one – as you've probably realised – and it's a reasonable argument that if you're the one uncomfortable with it, and it's only affecting you, then why should that also be your partner's problem? As I said, get a cleaner and recognise that you put the magazines and cushions straight because it's something you need to do for yourself.

## He or she is constantly criticising you

People who constantly criticise others are actually voicing their insecurities about themselves. It took an extreme example to demonstrate this to me when a very aggressive friend (by everyone's judgement of them) was the person who told me that I'm too aggressive, which was akin to Simon Cowell complaining that someone was insensitive with their feedback! You'll probably be able to see this with your own friends; the ones fighting their weight are most likely to be the ones who nag you about what you should and shouldn't eat, and the ones who overspend will be the ones most likely to question your spending habits and so on.

Just knowing this can make it much easier to deal with criticism but don't throw this knowledge back at your spouse. Instead try giving honest compliments. It may be exactly the opposite of what you want to do but when someone is full of praise for you the human response is to return it. We give what we receive. We get praise, we give praise. When we feel good about ourselves we are more likely to see the good in others.

If this doesn't work, and you're still suffering, address it head-on as calmly as you can: 'I do understand that you don't like my hair or dress sense. Can we agree to differ on this point and not raise it again as I feel very undermined and irritated when you keep mentioning it?' Your partner may not be aware how much and how often they're criticising you. Commonly they'll defend it by telling you that they're trying to help you. Make it clear that they're not helping, they're making things worse. If they don't stop tell them that you want to be with someone who loves you as you are, imperfections and all. Can they be that person?

## They've let themselves go (so you don't fancy/respect them any more)
Check first that you're not the villain of the previous problem. Is it you that's lost confidence and are turning that on to your spouse?

If you're sure that's not the explanation then find out why. It could be that they're depressed so they might need to see a doctor. Try and introduce a healthier lifestyle for yourself and ask them to come along to support you, making sure it's fun and not a chore. Go for walks, shop for clothes together. Give them loads of praise when they do look good or make an effort. 'Wow, you look gorgeous tonight.' Men need this just as much as women.

## Money

Arguments over money are usually because two people prioritise where money is spent differently, rather than over the lack of money. Sometimes the arguments are because one of you believes that the family income is yours only and that your partner should justify every penny they spend. It's a very common attitude when one partner is staying at home to care for children. Assuming it's been a joint decision for your partner to stay at home then legally and morally your partner has a right to your income. If it creates a divorce then you would be compelled by the courts to hand over money to maintain your family and would have no say in how it's spent.

To resolve both problems ensure that you each have your own bank accounts and that you also have a joint account. Make a budget together of all the things that you have to pay for every month including rent/mortgage, food, utility bills, children's pocket money, etc. Agree the contribution each of you make to those essentials (nothing if one of you doesn't earn) and ensure that sufficient money is transferred into the joint account from your personal accounts. Neither of you should use that joint account except for those essentials. If your partner is not earning you should also transfer an agreed amount into his or her personal account. Your partner should never have to ask for that money; it's demeaning and affects the delicate power balance in the relationship. What is left in your personal account is yours to spend however you wish. So, for example, if one of you likes to buy expensive food that doesn't come within the budget they should buy it out of their own money. If there's no money left for your personal accounts you need to look at ways of cutting back, realigning your debts, or increasing your income. But even a small amount of money that you know is 'yours' makes all the difference.

## They've started to drink heavily or take drugs

Drug and alcohol dependency (not use) are both symptoms of other problems such as depression or anxiety so you should try to get them to see a doctor. No one can tell or persuade someone else to give up; they have to be motivated to do so themselves. If they refuse any suggestion of treatment then you need to protect your family from the affects of the drug abuse ahead of trying to save the marriage. If the children are young then you should assume that they're not safe left in the addict's care. Whatever age they are the children will be terrified by the moods swings which go with both types of addiction; it's not something you should expose them to in their own home.

There are many support groups for families that can be found on the internet which are worth contacting. If you don't think your children are being affected by the addict's behaviour check the chat rooms of those aimed at children; you'll find it horrifying. My experience is that if you try to help an addict and stand by them while they refuse to admit that they have a problem, you're in effect colluding with them and encouraging them to do nothing. The ex-addicts I've known say that being ostracised by their families was the single most significant factor in their decision to become clean.

## The baby has changed how you feel about each other

Alarmingly the first year of a child's life is one of the most common times for a crisis in a marriage, with many men committing adultery or walking out during this time, so if this happens to you you're not alone.

The demands on a new mother, and on her body, can make it very difficult for her to give any attention to her husband. The husband can feel suddenly excluded: he was the centre of her world and now he comes a poor second.

It's also very common for one or both parents to find it much tougher than they were expecting to adapt to the interloper in their lives and the way it changes their relationship. When I talk to my childless friends I warn them that having children is like having an incontinent lodger who doesn't pay their way, demands you do everything for them, has a 'right' to your money and is impossible to evict for at least 18 years. It's not quite the romantic image that's usually presented. Of course, parenthood has huge rewards too, but the responsibility for many people comes as a sudden and shocking reality that they were not prepared for and makes some want to run.

Added to this the balance of power in your relationship will change. The carer will, probably for the first time, be dependent on their partner and interests will change quite dramatically. The one going out to work may have a false perception of what it's like to stay at home, contribute less to the chores and feel ownership of their income, so you have many of the problems listed under the money section of this chapter. You should recognise these feelings openly in conversation. Ensure that both of you has experience of staying at home for extended periods looking after a baby: a few hours is a very different experience to several days. They will then appreciate that it's much easier going out to work.

When I had my first child I thought that I would feed the baby, change it and put it down and then go back to sleep or get on with other things. You see new babies in TV dramas left contently in the corner while Mum gets on with her job, only pausing occasionally to feed the child. Of course the reality is very different and to make it worse, having failed to warn you how exhausting babies really are, these same people then tell you that the problems of being a parent never get easier, they just change. If that's the reason you feel like running, or are having fight after fight, I really sympathise, but wait. The first six weeks of the first child's life is easily the hardest part of being a parent. Things do get much easier, and even become enjoyable. I promise you.

## Your partner is too strict/too soft on the children

Whatever happens, your spouse will remain the children's parent, divorce won't change that, so ending your relationship because of differences in how you discipline your children will achieve nothing. Instead take some time to sit down to discuss and agree your rules and boundaries and then agree to stick to them. You'll both probably have to compromise but that's better for children than the confusion that different expectations will cause.

Never undermine each other in front of the children. It makes children very insecure. If you think your partner has been unfair say something to the child along the following lines; 'I'll check with Dad why he feels that you should be punished in that way. I'm sure he's only trying to be fair and ensure you understand that what you did was wrong.' Sometimes one parent's views on childcare are distorted because they don't know the child so well (and what they're capable of) and don't understand what it's like coping with a child all day every day. This can easily be corrected, and should be.

Neither of you can make rules unless you understand the child and the impact of enforcing them.

## Sex

The most common sexual problems are incompatible libidos, when one of you wants sex much more than the other one and a general boredom or disinterest (you stop fancying each other and the relationship has turned into one more like that of brother and sister).

There are a whole heap of issues that can be buried under those two headings. Sex can be both the cause and the symptom of other problems in the relationship, so it's not something to be ignored as isolated or trivial. Women often subconsciously turn off sex when they're angry or resentful towards their partner (see all the rest of the problems I've listed to get an idea what these might be). Men can feign indifference to sex if they have performance anxiety issues which could mean that they're having problems getting and/or maintaining an erection or can't climax. Many of these performance issues can be solved by going to the doctor and, for the sake of the marriage and however embarrassing it might be, he should see the doctor and be honest with his wife, who might otherwise think it's her fault. Contrary to the belief of many women, men going off sex is not likely to be an indication that he's 'getting it elsewhere'.

Men and women commonly base much of their own self-worth on their attractiveness to the opposite sex, so if one partner is refusing the other sex on a regular basis it's not just their physical needs that aren't being met; it impacts on their self-confidence as well. If you're telling your partner you don't want them physically any more then, however old you are, you're opening the door for someone else to come along and make your spouse feel attractive and good about themselves again. That's a very tough thing to turn down when the person at home deliberately makes them feel the opposite. The partner always refusing sex is breaking a marriage vow no less important to a good marriage than fidelity.

## Carl's story:

My wife went off sex soon after our second daughter was born. She'd never been very tactile or particularly affectionate with me but then she started to reject me totally. If we went away for the weekend she'd change in the bathroom and if I put my arm around her she'd pull away. I felt very frustrated sexually but it was the lack of any affection that really upset me. I would have been so happy if she'd even given me a hug occasionally. I tried everything, as I really wanted our marriage to work for our daughters, whom I love to bits, and in other respects the marriage was fine. I never cheated on her, even though it was obviously very tempting.

One day, after about 16 years of this treatment, I realised that I couldn't live like that any more. That was four years ago and she hasn't had a boyfriend since so I've started to think that it wasn't me she objected to but any form of physical affection. She's still upset I left her so it wasn't that she stopped loving me but I thought she must have at the time.

During a long-term relationship sex can get boring. If this is your problem then be creative in finding ways to spice things up. Start to put aside time and energy for your sex life; don't let it be an afterthought on a Saturday night when it feels like too much effort. Get romantic with each other again: go away, just the two of you, and dress up for each other like you would for a first date. If none of this works then the course of treatment that a counsellor is most likely to prescribe is celibacy. The two of you are banned from having sex for around two months. During that time you can gradually move though the bases, starting with just holding hands, through light kissing and petting, just like you did as teenagers. It sounds perverse but that's because human nature is perverse. If we can have something whenever we want it we don't want it any more. This method turns your partner into someone untouchable again. It also makes you explore other things, like kissing for hours, which you've probably not done for years. I'm always shocked by how many married people think it is strange to kiss their spouses; 'Well, you don't, do you?' one man told me. To which my answer was 'Why not? You should.' No wonder romance dies: go and give your spouse a really good snog and see what a dramatic difference it makes to how you feel about each other.

Relationship counsellors have a good success rate in solving sexual problems. If even the thought of speaking to someone else about your problems makes you blush then there are also some excellent books and websites that can help.

## The crisis points

Over time the problems build and can result in one or both of you discovering that you don't love or fancy your partner any more. This will lay the marriage open to a crisis point where you become so angry that you can't see a way for the marriage to continue.

The most common crises are caused by:

## Adultery – emotional and/or physical

It's difficult to be accurate but many studies suggest that more than 50 per cent of the population (both men and women) are likely to cheat on their long-term partner at some point in their lives. Whether this results in the end of your relationship will depend on your attitude to it, in terms of how significant you feel it is to your relationship, and the reasons for the adultery.

Some people are happy in open relationships and others don't see their partner's adultery as much more than irritating. There are a number of figures in the public eye, both men and women (though more commonly women), who live with their partner's repeated adultery and appear to remain happily married (although the media and society find this very difficult to accept).

At the other end of the scale some people will want to leave their spouse if they catch them flirting with someone else. There is no right or wrong way to be; it's a matter of your own emotional response to its significance. However you do need to understand where you are on that scale and understand why you feel like that before you can decide whether you'll be able to forgive and rebuild the marriage. This does assume that your spouse wants to remain married to you and still loves you. If not then there's little you can do, so brace yourself and ask.

I'm sure the biggest question on your mind is 'why?' Don't make assumptions, instead ask direct questions and get all the information you need. The adulterer probably won't want to give you the details to save you from further hurt but research suggests that without these details the victim of adultery will imagine worse. You need to know the truth to come to terms with it and use it to inform your judgement of whether to save the marriage or not.

Many people, particularly women, will immediately feel that the adultery has happened because the lover is more attractive than they are. It probably isn't true; look at celebrity marriages, the lover is often far less attractive or looks very similar to the spouse. This is mirrored in the experiences of the people I know. Instead the adultery usually occurs for emotional reasons. The most common are:

- Looking for attention and affection (they either need a lot or there is little in the marriage)
- Wanting a release from the stress of life at home (the affair exists in a fantasy world)
- Looking for reinforcement that they're attractive
- Drunken mistake/madness of the moment
- Looking for excitement (life can be boring; taking risks and having new sexual experiences can alleviate that boredom)
- Loneliness; either through lack of communication in the home or because of long and/or frequent time apart
- Mental illness making communication difficult, eg, Asperger's/autistic spectrum
- Physical illness making sex difficult, eg, degenerative illness such as MS or MND
- They genuinely fell in love

There are also many people who simply don't commit to monogamy, or even believe it's possible. If they were honest about that when they got married that's fine but if not it's clearly a fraudulent way to enter a marriage. If your spouse is arguing along these lines then they're giving you only two choices: leave or put up with their behaviour and not complain about it in future. Once you say you're leaving they may change their minds and make promises. If five minutes ago they didn't believe monogamy was possible, you threatening to leave may make them say something different, but it's not going to change their belief.

Some of the reasons for adultery are easier to forgive and forget than others. Rarely will people admit to some of them (for obvious reasons). However there are a few questions that will tell you the causes behind the adultery and will therefore help you understand whether you will be able to forgive it.

How many times did the adultery happen? A one-off incident is probably a moment of madness that is bitterly regretted. A year-long affair involves a lot of deceit and planning so hits more to the foundations of the marriage.

A man or woman who is a habitual flirt, even in front of their spouse, is likely to be looking for reinforcement that they're attractive and this is therefore unlikely to be an isolated incident.

You also need to know whether the adultery happened with one partner or more than one and whether they cheated in previous relationships.

If you're the adulterer don't think that lying will help save your marriage. To rebuild the marriage your spouse needs to know the truth. Without it, the two of you will not be able to address the issues behind what happened and your spouse will not have the information they need to decide what to do. Give your spouse all the details they ask, honestly. Don't complain if they keep raking up the past for many months. Keep answering their questions or they will imagine the worst. Don't lie, even to spare their feelings; they will quickly catch you out and that will make it far more difficult to rebuild trust. If your spouse starts spying on you, allow it and even encourage it. Leave your mobile phone lying around so that they can see text messages and your phone log. That will reassure them that you have nothing to hide.

Divorce statistics show that, although slightly more men than women cheat, men are less likely to be able to forgive it. It's believed that this is because women still 'accept' that men can't help being led astray by their libido whereas men still believe that women must be emotionally involved to have sex. Some men also still believe (usually subconsciously) that they 'own' their wives, so anyone else 'invading' his property is not just an emotional wound but one that hits right to male pride and ego.

The irony is that statistics also show that women are more likely to cheat for the sex and men for emotional reasons (to get more love) which is therefore pretty much the opposite of the assumptions that both genders make about each other. It also suggests that to get a man back a woman needs to show him a lot more affection and to get a woman back a man needs to reignite their sex life.

## A major fight where one of you has walked out and/or declared the marriage over

Don't do anything rash. Give yourselves time to calm down. Think of all those other times when you hated them and thought you'd never forgive them, yet you did. Whether you can move on from this will depend on the real cause of the fight. These can be one or a combination of the following:

- 'Kick the cat.' One of you has had a bad day and had to keep their temper with the people who caused the irritation. The bad mood then gets downloaded on to the first person available. This is often the person they love most because they feel safest with them.
- 'The straw that broke the camel's back.' Some people will tell you immediately if there's a problem (and are then regarded as easily irritated) and some will seethe inside for months until they explode – sometimes over something quite petty which can be very shocking to the partner, even if they were guilty of not treating their spouse fairly.
- Alcohol. Some people get argumentative and even violent every time they get drunk. There's an easy way to solve that one and if you know that's how alcohol affects you it's unfair to expose your family to it.
- 'The real thing.' This is a fight that stems from one of the issues that's causing real problems between you. It's likely that one or both of you thinks the other is taking advantage of them. If you can't sort it out yourselves you should see a relationship counsellor. These are the fights that will end a relationship if not resolved, as resentment will build.

Some people have 'happy' relationships where they argue passionately all the time. It's part of the excitement and drama of the marriage. That's fine between two consenting adults but you need to rethink it when you have children, as that sort of 'excitement' is emotionally scarring for children.

## Your spouse has committed an act that goes against your morals/belief system

It's very unlikely that your partner will have exactly the same moral standards as you on every issue; some couples are alarmingly different yet are happy, so this doesn't necessarily mean the end of the relationship. Your reaction will depend on the severity of the situation and whether the behaviour is typical or out of character.

## Your relationship has become physically violent

If your spouse is violent to you it's likely that at some stage they'll be violent towards the children. Don't fool yourself otherwise: it means they're either not in control of their anger or don't accept that this is a boundary that should not be crossed, so none of you are safe and you should remove your children from the situation immediately.

Someone who's never hit a person before and is genuinely sorry may be worth forgiving. Early on in a relationship it can be difficult to judge whether that's true. However the best indication is the type of person they've been before.

Have they tried to control you? Following incidents among my friends and family, and as the mother of two girls, I was very interested in learning how you can spot a potential abuser early on in a relationship. Many people leave it too late and are then emotionally and practically tied to the abuser. Abusers will also undermine their victims so much that they believe what the abuser is telling them and think they deserve it. These are the people who stay with the abuser when they should leave. So if your partner is apologising, and has never hit you before, run through this list, as it will give you a good indication of whether they're likely to be a threat to you again. Tick the ones that apply.

My partner:

- ☐ is jealous and possessive towards me
- ☐ tries to distance me from my friends and family
- ☐ belittles me constantly and criticises my looks, clothes, beliefs etc
- ☐ embarrasses me through jokes that demean and humiliate me in public
- ☐ pressures me into doing things that I don't want to do
- ☐ loses their temper quickly and inappropriately
- ☐ blames me when he or she has behaved badly towards me
- ☐ makes me worry about how they'll react to what I say and do
- ☐ tries to make me feel responsible for their emotional state
- ☐ keeps track of my time and/or the amount of my money I spend
- ☐ doesn't respect my personal property (destroys it or takes it)

The more you answer yes the quicker you need to get out (though a tick beside even one of these points should give you serious cause for concern). Of course, if you're always overspending and running up debts or have been caught cheating in the past (for example) then it's far more normal for your partner to check up on you.

Also consider whether your partner has always been like this or whether they've changed. Some of the symptoms could be due to mental illnesses such as bipolar (often known as manic depression) or obsessive compulsive disorder (OCD). If it's the result of depression then it may well be treatable.

# The effect of children's age

You may have read all the above and decided that you can stay together for the sake of the children. You think you can, like many do, live in a marriage that bores you without showing any symptoms to your children. You can continue to be good, supportive parents together while no longer having any interest in each other. If that's you then you need to think seriously about whether you're really prepared to make that sacrifice and how long for: for ever or until they reach a certain age? What age will it affect them least?

The most surprising thing I learnt in researching this book is that it's better not to make the sacrifice at all unless you can make it for ever. The older the 'children' are the worse it seems to affect them and when saying that I'm including adults in their 20s and 30s.

### Mark's story:

Twenty years ago my then wife left me with four children of varying ages from 2 to 13 years. The amount the divorce affected my children directly correlated with how old they were at the time. The older they were the worse they seem to have suffered.

There is no 'easy' age for children, although the age of the children may affect what you decide to do and how you handle the situation.

## Babies

If your children are under two years old then you can assume that they'll not remember this time in their lives and they're likely to quickly settle into new routines. On the downside it means that they will never experience having both their parents together and will grow up with the uncertainty of how they fit into whatever new family is created. These children also suffer most from never growing up in an intact household. This can be very tough and is covered in Chapter 6 on establishing new families.

Even if they're unaware of what's happening babies will pick up on tension in the house so may be much more restless than normal. Their progression may seem to halt a little; eg, refusing solid food after they're weaned. They'll therefore need lots of cuddles and reassurance and, like you would with older children, try not to let them hear you fight.

## Toddlers

As a toddler's vocabulary develops they will understand the fights between you. They will also have some concept of what a fight is and what anger is. They will be very familiar with how angry they are during a tantrum and the fact it passes. Speak to them and reassure them in language they understand. 'You get really mad with Mummy sometimes but you don't always feel like that, do you? Mummy and Daddy feel like that sometimes with each other; but that doesn't make it something that you need to be scared of, does it?' Like babies, they will probably show that they're unsettled by becoming more irritable, tantrums may increase and they could revert to more baby-like behaviour.

The separation will affect them more than the divorce, as they won't understand the finality of divorce; what will matter to them is if one of their beloved parents is not at home any more. However, like babies, they will soon settle into a new routine.

### Eleanor's story:

My husband left me for another woman when our sons were two and four years old. The good thing about them being so young was that they keep me busy so I've had no time to feel sorry for myself.

I took the oldest boy to family counselling, really as a cautionary measure, as I was affected badly by my parents' divorce, and that's worked really well. I didn't bother with the younger one as I assumed that he wouldn't ever find it a problem as he was so young when his father left. However now, two years on, he's started asking questions about it: 'Why doesn't Daddy love you any more?' and saying things like, 'I'd like Daddy to live with us; that would be nice, wouldn't it, Mummy?' However I think they're both coming through it fine and are very happy but I would urge other parents not to assume that the children won't be affected, however young they are.

## Young schoolchildren

At this age they will need reassurance that they will still have the love and protection they need whatever happens, and that they're not going to lose one of you. A few days in a very young child's life is a long time so unless there is a danger that they will hear something try to delay telling them about the separation until the practical arrangements are being made. However if one child is older it would be unfair to expect him or her to keep the secret from younger siblings.

It's worth letting your children's teacher know about the problems at home. It's not uncommon for children to restrain themselves at home (for fear of redirecting the anger they sense to them) and to release that emotion at school in behaviour such as bullying. If the teachers are aware they can ensure that they keep alert to possible problems and deal particularly sensitively to minor infringements of rules, eg, if you've just told your child that you're separating and they forget their homework the next day a punishment is unfair.

Even at this age you're unlikely to be the first parents to separate. If possible see if you can arrange play dates with children whose parents seem to have split amicably. As adults we tend to seek support from others who've experienced the same problems. Children will also find comfort in being able to express their worries to someone who's been through it and come out the other side without the world ending.

## Teenagers

It's now been established that, due to the brain's efforts to change a child into an adult, teenagers are much less able to empathise with people during puberty than either younger children or adults. They will consequently make your life tough even if you have a loving, supportive partner; if you have struggles of your own, your house could quickly turn into a war zone.

Teenagers tend to think that they're the centre of the world so they will assume, even more than younger children, that the problems their parents have are about them in some way. They might have the attitude that parents have no 'right' to separate and try to make you feel very guilty about how selfish you are. They might even suggest that you're doing it just to upset them (seriously!). Teenagers like to think that they have the monopoly on being upset and bad-tempered so they probably won't have a lot of sympathy to spare for you. The only way to deal with problems in your marriage when you have teenagers is to keep as united a front as possible or, very quickly, teenagers will play one of you off against each other, which will make your life hell.

Despite their 'cool' or aggressive appearance, teenagers can be as scared and upset as younger children. Try to give them lots of attention, however much you think they don't want it, and sit down as often as you can to talk to them seriously about what's happening. As you come to decisions, involve them and let them have some say. Teenagers think they're adults so the one thing guaranteed to make them mad is if you decide things for them.

I've found that teenagers need much more affection, attention and demonstration that they're loved than toddlers. They'll say they don't want it, and don't need you, but they're the most isolated age group in many ways. As a child we get hugs all the time from our parents, as adults we have our partner to hug, but teenagers are too cool to admit to needing affection. So try lots of hugs in private (when no one else, not even a sibling, is around). If they really won't accept a hug give them affection in other ways. Praise (honest and not over the top) and lots of attention will both go some way to helping them cope.

Teenagers can surprise you: some will not be bothered by your separation, they've seen it all before, and they don't really think it will affect them. Double-check that they really do feel like this, then be grateful and don't try and to force them to be unhappy about it (see the final chapter).

## Children who are not children

You probably think that if you have children who are over 18, particularly if they're now away from home, that you can separate without giving them too much thought. You'd be very wrong.

### Tina's story:

On the day I got my A level results my parents congratulated me and then told me that they'd been waiting for this day to separate. They didn't separate before because they thought they should stay together for my sake. Instead they chose the day I'd worked hard for two years towards, the day when I started worrying about the reality of leaving home for university and the day I should be celebrating. They took all that away from me. I really couldn't believe their timing. I think it was pretty unforgivable.

Many older children believe that, if you've managed to live together all these years, you should be able to just carry on. Divorce will still rock their world as much as when they were dependent on you. Children as old as 30 were the ones who seemed to be hit hardest and took longest to come to terms with it. In fact, I failed to get many of this group to talk to me, as even five years on they still felt it was 'too raw'.

As I said at the beginning, there is no good age to get divorced from a child's viewpoint.

### Harry's story:

Our marriage had been dead for years but we stayed together until our youngest, Siobhan, had left and gone to university and then we had an amicable separation. I found it a huge relief. However Siobhan began to show serious signs of anxiety. She pretty much refused to travel on public transport, which made university life very difficult for her, and she wouldn't even consider going on holiday with her friends.

She pretended to me that it didn't bother her but eventually we referred her to counselling, which naturally was confidential, so it was some time before I discovered the problem. I had casually told Siobhan one day that the reason why her mother and I had separated after being married so long was because we felt it right that we should wait until all the children left home. This made her feel incredibly guilty. She also felt that her foundations, her home with us, was shaken at the same time as she was only just starting to learn to live without our day-to-day support and living away for the first time. This combination had caused her mental health problems.

I was really shocked until I spoke to a university professor who told me that the most common need for counselling at university was for students whose parents had done exactly the same as us: waited until the youngest child was at university before separating. The students found it incredibly tough. I've since spoken to friends who divorced when their children were in their late 20s and experienced similar problems.

## Expectations after the divorce

You should think seriously about what you hope and expect to gain from the divorce. Do you imagine that life after divorce will be wonderful; freedom from monotony and hot new lovers every night?

Without children, divorce can be straightforward, as you can quickly rebuild your life. With children, things are far more complicated and life is likely to be rocky for a while until you manage to get everyone settled into the new life again. It might take years before you're even happy again and it's nearly always much tougher than people imagine it will be. You'll have less money, no one to lean on emotionally and financially and you'll be responsible for lives that need rebuilding. You won't have time or energy to consider your own love life for some time. You're throwing all the pieces of your life up into the air without knowing where they'll fall. Wendy's comments are typical, 'I was just so relieved to get out of a relationship that I was totally disinterested in entering a new one.'

The arguments you're having now with your spouse will continue, unless you both agree to put them behind you. You'll also be adding new arguments and problems.

Dating again, particularly after being married for any length of time, is truly horrendous. Someone changed all the rules in the 1980s and 1990s and didn't tell me. You may think you're a confident, mature person but the horrors of meeting new potential partners and being rejected will be as bad as when you were a teenager (see Sex as a single parent on page 169).

## Have a test run

If you've stayed at home to look after the children, and you know that you'll need to work again, it's better to find a job and start it before you separate. That way your children will have a chance to get used to you not being around so much before the stress of the divorce, and you'll begin to get an idea of the practical problems of working and caring for children.

Find out what it's like not to be a couple before you make the break. I found it surprisingly common for people to quickly realise they'd made a mistake but it was then too late to go back to what they had. Take your children on holiday without your partner, and get him or her to do the same at a later date. Tell your children you couldn't get the time off together. This will give you a good idea what it's like managing without your partner and what it's like being single. Find a place where you can get babysitters some nights and go out on your own. Experience again the cattle market of not having a partner on your arm. It will either make you run back to your marriage or want to break free even more, but at least you'll have a much better idea of what the reality will be like.

## The importance of space

It is common for one partner to want the separation and divorce and the other to be unwilling or fearful to give them the space and time they need to make a decision. Instead they spoil their spouse, they beg and use any emotional blackmail they can think of (even if they don't consciously give it that label) in an attempt to 'fight' to save the marriage. That behaviour usually makes the partner who wants the separation feel crowded and creates an even stronger desire to get away from the marriage. If that sounds like your marriage try and remember the games you had to play when you were dating; now is no different. The cooler you are about things, the more you keep out of their way, the more chance you have to make them realise they would miss you. Obviously this doesn't apply if your spouse wants the divorce because they feel unloved.

### Christine's story:

My then husband Graeme and I agreed that I should go alone on the cruise we'd booked to give me the chance to decide whether the marriage was really over. But Graeme couldn't give me even that space and joined me as a 'romantic surprise' at the second port. I was furious and it was that action which decided things in my head. How could I stay with someone who wouldn't even respect my wishes at such a critical time?

## To break or not to break?

Remember, it is not what your spouse has done that will cause you to divorce; it will be your reaction to it. However your relationship is probably beyond saving if:

- One of you refuses to give up a lover despite the other knowing about it and demanding it
- You've not been in love with each other for 18 months or more
- You feel embarrassed when people see you together

- You can't even be bothered to argue with your spouse any more
- One of you has admitted to being gay
- He or she is violent or abusive towards you and/or the children
- Your spouse makes you feel bad about yourself and who you are

Your relationship might be saved if:

- The desire for divorce has come after a big fight
- One of you has cheated but is genuinely sorry
- You're going through a bad patch but this time last year things were fine
- You still love each other

If you decide you can stay together and rebuild things, do check you're succeeding and not fooling yourselves. One of the worst mistakes you can make is leaving the separation until you both become so bitter against each other that it makes an amicable separation almost impossible. Some people will also assume things are fine because that makes them feel safe again. Brace yourself and check with your spouse before making that assumption and don't slip back into bad habits.

# Chapter 2

---

## Telling the Children and Handling Their Pain

---

- How and when to tell them
- Likely questions
- What is it about divorce that hurts children?
- First-stage rules
- Arguing in front of children
- Behaviour
- Emotions
- The day
- Other people

Telling someone you don't love them any more and seeing their face collapse into grief is the toughest thing most people ever have to do; that is until you have to sit your children down and tell them that you're going to rip their life in two and that they will never live in the security of a united family, with the people they love, ever again. Even at his or her point of worst despair your spouse will have some hope that they can replace what they're losing, even if they deny it. Your children will never be able to have back what you're taking from them and they'll know that.

### Sue's story:

I wanted the split; my husband didn't, so he told me I had to tell the children that night. It was terrible; he was in tears in the living room and both our sons were in their rooms. I told our elder son first and he burst into loud sobs which meant by the time I got to our younger son he was terrified. His first reaction was to angrily push me away and neither of them asked many questions. With the whole house sobbing, I went to sit on our bed by myself. I lay there listening to everyone crying and wailing. I believed I was the most selfish mother ever: I was the person who'd just destroyed three lives. I've never felt so bad about anything I've done either before or since. We're now all happy, and wouldn't have been if we'd stayed married, but I still shudder at that memory.

How can you tell your children sensitively and address their concerns and needs?

## How and when to tell them

Your children will probably remember the moment you tell them that you're separating for the rest of their lives. It's therefore something that needs careful thought and preparation; you don't want them to find out from someone else, or worse, in the heat of an argument, eg, 'Your father doesn't want us any more.' Your children will try very hard to find out why. It's unlikely, particularly if they're very young, that they'll have had any idea that this was going to happen, even if you've been arguing a lot or one of you has been violent towards the other, so be prepared for their shock.

## The don'ts:

- Don't approach your children until you're absolutely sure that this is the end; it's not something you want them worrying about unnecessarily
- Don't assume that because your children are older that they'll not be as deeply affected (the reverse is usually true)
- Don't use the opportunity to get your side of the argument across to your children or paint your spouse as the villain (even if you think they are)
- Don't use your children to argue the case for keeping the family together. It's a terrible burden to put on them, sets unrealistic expectations that they can 'save their lives' and is emotional blackmail against your spouse. And do you really want to be married to someone who's only with you because your children begged them?
- Don't do it in a public setting or in front of other relatives or friends. This is a private moment; your children will probably be distressed and no one likes breaking down in front of other people
- Don't try and defend your actions or get into an argument about it

- Don't expect to be asked questions straightaway, they may need time to take it in
- Don't leave it to your spouse to handle alone; your children may want to speak to you too
- Don't avoid telling them and just disappear one day; it's not like ripping off a plaster; you need to let them get used to the idea before one of you leaves the home
- Don't blame them, or suggest you blame them, in any way
- Don't assume that they're going to be devastated and encourage that emotion; be prepared for it but also accept that children react in different ways and some may actually be relieved, particularly if you've been fighting a lot

Some of these may sound obvious but they're all based on real-life accounts.

If you have more than one child make sure they all find out from you and not from each other or from listening at doors. This will give them a distorted idea of what's going to happen, and because you've not discussed it openly they're likely to feel less able to tell you their worries and concerns.

I found it alarmingly common for one or both parents to tell their children that they'd always been unhappy in the marriage. If you tell your children that it makes them question their whole childhood up to that point and their part in your unhappiness. You're effectively telling them that all those times that they felt they were in a happy family, those magical days out and those cosy times in, were all a lie. Children find that very difficult to deal with and they'll be very suspicious of happiness in future. They might also feel guilty if they think you only stayed together for their sake. Children want to look back and think that they were part of a happy family. Don't take that away from them.

## The dos:

- Try to get each child on his or her own and out of earshot of the others. This should be one-to-one or two-to-one (with both parents there) if possible so that they feel free to ask questions and have your complete attention
- Be loving and affectionate; recognise and accept their pain (but don't anticipate or encourage it if it's not there)
- Reassure them of your love and of the love of your spouse for them (if he or she isn't with you)
- Reassure them that you'll both stay part of their lives
- Promise them that you'll never stop them seeing and spending time with each of their parents
- Promise them that you will stay as friendly as you can to each other
- Be prepared to answer their questions, and also for their refusal to talk about it
- Be ready to come back to the subject when they're ready
- Make what you say age appropriate
- Be there for them: choose a time when you don't have to rush off to do something else
- Let them be by themselves if they want to be:

some children will want to grieve in private before
they're ready to talk to you
- Be as honest as you can be with them. It's good to
let them know you're upset but try to cut out the
bitterness you feel

### Carl's story (continued):

My wife insisted I told our daughters who were both in
their late teens. My younger daughter screamed at me
and I put my arms around her to tell her that I would still
be there for her and that she wasn't losing me. That
same daughter quickly accepted the break-up and
within weeks told me that the separation was good
because it meant she was now part of the 'in crowd' of
children from broken homes like all her friends.

## Likely questions

The first reaction is likely to be shock, tears and anger but this
can vary hugely and your children might even appear disinterested.

Your children may reject any comfort you try to give them.
At some point they will probably start asking questions.
Think about how you answer them as it will set the scene for
how supported they feel during the divorce. Most children
are not deaf or stupid and if you assume they are you're likely
to make them question the trust they have in you. Don't lie
unless you really have to, as children know you very well and
will probably recognise when you're lying, or have overheard
the truth in arguments (see below: Arguing in front of children), and this will set up mistrust.

A mother, two years after her divorce, was asked by her young son, 'Daddy told me something different to what you told me; one of you is lying. Is it you or is it Daddy?' Whatever the mother answered to this question, the child would have made his own judgement based on what he saw and what he heard and it's very likely that he would have quickly found out the truth. How do you think he then felt about the parent who had lied to him?

The most likely questions are variations on the following and even if they don't ask them it's probably what will be on their mind so you should address them:

## Why?

I don't think you should go into detail, as this is likely to cause your bitterness to rise to the surface but they do need to have some idea or they will make wild guesses. Agree the answer with your spouse first and keep it to something along the lines of 'We make each other unhappy and we don't want that to start to affect you.' Over time more details will come out, such as who instigated the divorce, but over time those details matter less as shock and anger fade and they begin to see that life does go on.

If one of you is going to live with someone else straight away then you obviously need to warn them and give that as the reason. Your children are likely to blame this person and the adulterer but the other spouse should discourage it (despite the fact that you probably agree with them). Your aim is to find a way for your children to continue a relationship with both their parents and encouraging that sort of animosity and blame will make that much more difficult. So however hard it is, do what you can to encourage your children to maintain a good relationship with your ex and build a relationship with their new partner, who will become an important part of their lives.

## Where will we live?/What will happen to us?

This is your chance to find out what's important to them so that you can come to arrangements that suit them. Stress that whatever you decide will be based around their needs and that both of you love them so much that you will want to make sure you see lots of them still.

## Will there be lots of fighting?

Be honest with your children that things will be tense but promise them that you'll both try to minimise any arguments, because you recognise that it's not fair on them. Unfortunately your children will probably have picked up their ideas about divorce from television and friends. Both of these dramatise things and so will give them a distorted view of how bad things are going to get. They may, for example, believe that the two of you are going to start screaming at each other the whole time and throwing things about, even if you've not done that before. You need to explain to them that television programmes have to be dramatic and show things as nasty as possible in order to make you want to keep watching them. People would not be interested in a storyline where two characters have an amicable divorce. Similarly friends do not bother telling us about things that are going fine in their lives. 'Fine' is boring and doesn't make for good gossip. People will pour out their troubles, when they have troubles, but not usually bother giving you an update when things are going well.

The younger your children are the easier it is for them to completely misunderstand things, but that can happen at any age. To avoid this you need to actively listen to any comments they have about the divorce to ensure that they've not misunderstood anything and correct them straight away.

### Margaret's story:

My ex and I split because we just couldn't get on. We were always irritated with each other but we tried to keep things amicable and were careful to talk about it with our children. However, when Charlotte, who was 13, had friends round one day I was putting the washing away and overheard her talking to her friend. It was clear from what she was saying that she believed that the separation was her fault and she based this on something she'd overheard in one of our arguments. Like most teenagers, she wasn't always easy to live with but I really don't know what we could have said to make her think that. I was pretty sure that we'd told her that she wasn't to blame.

# What is it about divorce that hurts children?

To avoid the long-term damage that many children suffer as a direct result of their parents' divorce, you'll find it helpful to know what the likely problems will be so that you can plan against them now. This will also help you understand why I make the suggestions I do in later chapters. The most commonly cited issues can be summarised under the following headings:

## Children of divorced parents can find it difficult to trust in love and believe they can go on to have happy long-term relationships

This is not my experience; perhaps things really have moved on so much, and divorce is so common that the breakdown of relationships is now accepted as a natural feature of them that needn't be feared. Less than 50 per cent of us will achieve happy long-term relationships but recognition of this doesn't, in my experience, stop us striving for them and finding loving relationships worthwhile, whether they go the distance or not. I think that's the message we should help children understand in divorce: 'We married; it didn't work out but we're still glad we got married as we've had some lovely times and, best of all, we produced you.' Adopting that attitude may help prevent you feeling bitter about it too.

None of us can take our partners for granted and assume we will be with them until one of us dies so, to turn this on its head, it's possible that children who reach adulthood with happily married parents might go into marriage without the understanding that there is a very high chance that things will go wrong. I've also heard friends, who have happily married parents, say that they haven't got married because they've never found a relationship as good as the one their parents have.

Children will learn from you how to have relationships and what to avoid, so if you're setting a bad example in your married life, that can be worse for children than seeing you go through an amicable divorce. However if your divorce is a terrifying experience for them, where the two of you take your gloves off and hurt each other as much as possible, you shouldn't be too surprised if your children grow up frightened of trusting anyone with their love.

## Eve's story:

My father is very controlling and my memories of my childhood are of being scared of him as he ranted and raved at pretty much everyone. The person who usually got the worst of it was my mum and he regarded me as his favourite (and openly admitted it), so I used to come off fairly lightly. My parents stayed together though and have just celebrated 60 years of 'married bliss'.

I'm hopeless in relationships and treat men really badly. My first-ever boyfriend waited patiently for two years before I was ready for sex and then for the mandatory two weeks for the pill to be safe; but the week before, I slept with his best friend. It's taken me years, and quite a bit of professional help, to work out why I behave like that. I never want to risk trusting a man, or relying on him emotionally, so I keep the upper hand by being the one to let the relationship down. The person who loves most loses all power in the relationship so I have to prove to myself that I'm not the powerless one; like my mum was with my dad. I'm now in my 40s, divorced with two children, and I still do it; I'm cheating on the guy I'm seeing now. I'm sure he's cheating on me so it evens the score, even if he doesn't know it. My boyfriend wants us to live together but giving up that sort of power to another man is not something I'm willing to do again. I left my husband because he started to remind me of my father.

## Children of remarried families are not as close to their parents

This is real danger in stepfamilies, particularly if new children are born into them. This is the 'wicked stepmother' syndrome where the new step-parent appears, at best, to be competing for time with the natural parent and, at worst, to be actively pushing the children of the previous marriage away. Abuse, in all its forms, is far more common by step-parents towards children than any other group. Stepfamilies need to be handled very carefully if they're to be successful and avoid making children from the previous relationship feel like unloved orphans who are nothing more than a horrible reminder of a mistake. The subject is dealt with in detail in Chapter 6 but if you're going straight into a new family read quickly to get there.

Children of divorced parents who don't remarry appear to be much closer to each other. That's explored more in the final chapter.

## Children whose parents divorced learn that feelings are painful and hide from them

My daughters are now old enough to form relationships and I've seen no evidence of a fear of getting hurt; when I checked with them they both laughed at the idea and gave me a heap of evidence that proved that they weren't just trying to reassure me.

However many of the most conscientious parents (which probably includes you, as you took the trouble to buy this book) now make such an effort to keep things amicable and avoid any display of emotion that children can gain the impression that emotions should be buried and that it's wrong to show them. This doesn't help them learn how to handle feelings as a normal part of life. The handling of emotions is therefore dealt with later in this chapter. It's not simply a matter of keeping yourself in check, as is commonly assumed.

## Parents reduce the quality of their care when they get divorced

Many of the issues raised by divorce are difficult to handle because you're relying on someone else's behaviour. This one is entirely in your gift to get right. You should aim to ensure that your children feel at least as well parented after the divorce as they feel now and that you don't get distracted by new partners, the opportunity to party or the pressures of your new life.

The amount of care a child needs obviously depends on their age. After separation or divorce you should try to increase the care available rather than decrease it. It's a time when they'll feel vulnerable and need more proof than normal that they have parents who are there for them and who are not too caught up in their own lives to give them the attention and security they need. Tips on how to increase care are handled in Chapter 5.

In the first flush of freedom many divorcees make the most of their new single status by enjoying a party lifestyle which can include getting drunk, being out late and bringing friends back to the home who are strangers to their children. Remember that children need babysitters, your home is their home too and that drinking too much and staying out late does not mean you're excused from the school run in the morning. You're not the single, responsibility-free person you were before you had children and acting like you are will have consequences for them emotionally. Your first priority should remain your role as parent and any partying you do should fit around that and not diminish the stability of the home nor the quality of the care your children receive, particularly in the early months of your separation. You'll also be setting an example to your children and will undermine your authority with them if they see you acting irresponsibly. That doesn't mean you should become a martyr to your children, just that you don't get carried away with your new freedom. This is dealt with in more detail in Chapter 5.

## Divorce creates economic hardship

The poorest families in developed countries are almost always those where there is only one parent. It's not difficult to work out why: one household divided into two will mean that both are poorer. Money worries are likely to make you irritable with your children when you need to be calm and is likely to spark off fighting with your ex at the time you need to move on. Make sure, before you split, that you know exactly what your monthly income and outgoings will be and (if you're buying and selling property) try to leave yourself enough in savings so that in the immediate aftermath of the separation you're not worrying about money.

You may find that your new household income and/or situation makes you eligible for state benefit so it is worth contacting your local benefits office to ascertain exactly what you're entitled to.

Some parents will try and use financial hardship as another way of trying to punish their ex through the children. Typically this will mean that any cuts they make to the budget will be concentrated on the areas that will hurt the children most, for example, taking them out of private schooling just before exams or curtailing activities that are their obsessions. They will even pretend to themselves that they had no choice and their ex is the villain in the situation. Obviously be very careful that this isn't you, because you know who the real villain in that scenario is.

In many households the separation will mean that there are things that the children won't be able to do any longer. Budget carefully, be sensitive to your children's needs and dreams and, in simple language they understand, give them some say over what the cuts are. Some people like to protect their children from the harsh realities of budgeting but I believe it's another skill that needs to be developed as early as possible so you shouldn't feel guilty or embarrassed about it. When very young that means avoiding waste, as they get older they need to develop an understanding that everything comes at a price and you have to make choices and prioritise in order to stay within budget. That lesson does not mean making them share the burden of worrying whether you're going to be able to pay the rent.

Finally it is still depressingly common for one parent to try to evade financial responsibility for their children, which often results in needlessly plunging the children into poverty. However angry you are with your ex and however much you want to punish them, even if they're failing to let you see your children, it is never morally justifiable to fail to pay your share of your children's upkeep. I was shocked by how many otherwise thoughtful and intelligent parents failed to pay child maintenance when they got into disputes with their ex.

# First-stage rules

At this early stage you need to agree some headline rules between you and your ex to help you handle this very tense period. I suggest you leave the detail of the rule setting until you've actually separated as you'll then be in a better position to understand the issues more clearly. More detailed advice on setting rules is contained in Chapter 4. I would suggest you agree now that:

- You both remain responsible for your children. Neither should take it on themselves to make major decisions without the other being involved.

You should start planning now, before you split, for the future and how things will be. In order to set in everyone's mind the idea that you're both responsible for the children (even if one of you hasn't had much of a role until now) it's a good idea to start to think about who will be responsible for what in future. If you don't one of you will, in effect, become a single parent by default, carrying an unfair share of the burden. An example is the routine appointments and check-ups children need. One of you should make sure the children see the dentist regularly and the other the optician. This doesn't necessarily mean that the appointments should always come on that person's 'shift', just that they take responsibility for them happening and assume that they will take the children. It's these little things that can get forgotten and which demonstrate to children that they're still cared about and that life goes on.

- Neither of you are allowed to criticise or mock the other (or their new partner) in front of your children: that includes minimising arguments between the two of you in their presence.

How would you feel if someone was being rude about your best friend in front of you? That's how your children will feel when they hear their other parent criticised. Relatives and friends can also be at fault here so you should be proactive in stopping it when you hear it. Remember that even very young children have ears. I know many children who've had to listen to one parent be very rude about the other and they all report it as one of the worst experiences of the divorce. It makes children feel disloyal if they don't defend the other parent but frightened at the prospect of stepping in. The result is commonly a huge anger towards the parent who's done this to them. Please note celebrity couples who give interviews that create headlines such as: 'My ex-husband made my life hell.'

You should decide now on the future communications channels between you. Don't assume you can discuss issues between you (such as maintenance payments) as you hand over your children. This is a stressful time for them and hearing your continued squabbles, however you phrase things, will make things much worse for them. Don't ever cut off communication between you or leave it in the hands of the lawyers or the children. There are going to be many issues which you will need to agree jointly and there will be times ahead where you need to act as a united parenting force again. If things are very bitter between you, meet on neutral territory, such as a café, where you can't scream at each other.

## Arguing in front of children

One of the most painful things for your children during this time will be the arguments between you, and there are likely to be many as you both battle with the emotional and practical fallout from the announcement that you're going to split.

Try to avoid arguing in front of the children. I'm sure you can remember how awful that felt when you were a child. You're their security. Without you they're alone in the big, bad, frightening world. Listening to your heated arguments can seriously disrupt children, causing everything from bed-wetting (even in quite old children) to criminal behaviour. They're not going to believe that you'll have an amicable divorce where they'll be able to spend time with both of you and life will be secure again if the two of you are hurling abuse at each other every night.

Your separation is going to fundamentally affect their lives so there is a good chance that your children will actively try to find out as much as possible about it through whatever means they can. Wouldn't you in their position? The chances of them spying on your arguments are therefore very high. My own children recently admitted to sitting on our landing, listening to what we were saying. My elder daughter apparently kept the younger one quiet, stopped her going downstairs and gave her the signal to flee to her room when there was any danger that they would be found out. You therefore need to be very careful what you say to each other. If you tell them that you're divorcing because you've grown apart but you then have an argument, even in hushed voices, about the adultery that's the real cause, your children will probably know about it.

Some people say really evil things to each other when they've lost their temper, such as 'I wish you were dead'. It's not acceptable however angry or drunk you are and if you do it then make sure you apologise to your spouse and your children and emphasise that that's not how you really feel.

A degree of dissent and disagreement however is part of everyday life; if they never experience it as a child they will find it very disturbing as an adult. Children also need to learn how to argue, and they'll pick that up from you. If you find yourself arguing make it a rule that you:

- Don't use abusive language
- Don't let it get violent
- Don't scream at each other
- Allow the other person to put across their view-point
- Ask questions to help you understand the other person's viewpoint
- Never involve the children in any way. It is totally unfair to ask, for example, for a child's view on who's right
- Don't bring irrelevant historical crimes up
- Don't lie to support your arguments

If you've argued in front of the children ensure that the children also see you apologising to each other, particularly if you broke any of the rules above. This will help them to understand that arguments are part of life, not the end of the world.

Giving feedback is a far more constructive way of arguing and, if you can manage it in the heat of the moment, will make a huge difference to achieving a better degree of understanding between you. To do it you simply take away the focus of your comments from their behaviour and your speculation about what that behaviour means. This usually includes some exaggeration to emphasise the point and your annoyance, eg, 'You always turn up late just to annoy me and upset the children because we don't matter any more!'.

Instead, you can explain how that behaviour makes you feel, recognising that those feelings may be a misunderstanding of what that person intended and that they're probably struggling too, eg, 'I know life is very busy for both of us right now but when you're late I lose time waiting for you and can't do all the things I need to. That makes me tenser than I'd otherwise be when you do arrive and your lateness makes the children think they're less important to you than other things in your life. Is there any chance you could warn me when you've been delayed, or should we simply find a time that suits you better?'

The first statement is likely to get a defensive response that throws the accusation back at you, eg, 'I'm not always late, and so what, I'm busy, thanks to all your demands.' The second example gets to the real reason for your annoyance; it recognises that the other person is struggling too and most importantly suggests a choice of constructive solutions to the problem. That changes the focus from you accusing him or her to vent your anger, to finding a way forward that suits both of you.

Remember too that we all flit between three characters: parent, adult and child. Talk to someone as an adult and they will respond as an adult (the second example), talk to them like a parent and they'll probably respond in the immature emotional way of a child (the first example). Arguments are always more productive if you keep them adult to adult. You'll probably want to let off steam and really let rip with your anger sometimes (I'm sure that's not just me) but it will backfire if you do that now with your spouse. Now's the time to take up kick-boxing or something else that's suitably aggressive but both legal and safe. Treat the relationship with your spouse with the same care you would the relationship you have with your boss or anyone else you have to get on with.

One tip for taking the heat out of arguments is to swap sides. It's a tool they use at law schools to train them because a lawyer's job is to argue points whether they agree with them or not. In the middle of an argument, where you're getting nowhere, stop and each has to argue from the other one's viewpoint. If things are too emotional it may be something you do with a friend later. It sounds daft but do try it; it may even make you laugh. I've done it a couple of times and after the initial 'I've got no good points to make, I'm just being selfish and greedy' type line you quickly get into the spirit of it and start to see things differently. You may well find that your natural competitiveness kicks in and you start to really try to 'win' it for the other side.

# Behaviour

It's very likely that the stress you've put your children under will show in some changes in their behaviour.

## Too good
Despite the popular media image of children, many are such good little souls that they'll be very worried about both of you, whatever their age. They'll know you're hurting and they'll want to make it better; it's also one way that they demonstrate that they blame themselves, which I mentioned earlier. They might even think that if they're really good the two of you will love each other again and everything will be all right. You might suddenly find a tiny helper in the kitchen, rooms being cleaned and breakfast being presented to you

both in bed. It's difficult not to weep when a small child tries to put right an adult problem like this. Of course you should encourage good behaviour and reward it, but you also need to sit the child down and make sure they understand that it's not their behaviour that's caused the split and it's very unlikely that you'll get back together again. Use it as an opportunity to reassure them about life after the divorce and what it'll be like.

## Too bad

With the exception of some remarkably calm individuals, that I've read about in books but never met, people who've had a bad day or are upset or worried about something tend to be irritable with other people and less inclined to bother with them and what they want. Children are no different, so some deterioration in behaviour is to be expected during this turbulent and worrying time in their lives. It's tempting to let the rules slip: you're preoccupied with other emotions yourself and you feel sorry for them and want to keep things as happy as possible. To some degree that's fine; don't feel you have to enforce every minor rule but be aware of the message you're giving them if you let things slide too much.

The structure of your children's lives is something that the divorce threatens and discipline is an important part of that. Reminding children that the structures are still there will be reassuring for them, however much they might claim the opposite. So although it's a good idea to recognise that they will be bad tempered sometimes, and need to be left to get over it, on the bigger issues stand firm, together. I'm sure you already know that many children will push you as far as they can to test you. They will complain loudly that you're overly strict but children recognise, whatever age they are, that their friends who are allowed to do whatever they want are the ones whose parents don't care. What children say and what they think are different things. The daughter of a friend stupidly once admitted to her mum that she thought she was a 'pushover' compared to her dad. This, despite moaning frequently before and since that the mother was too strict. So don't be fooled into thinking you're being mean; if they moan just tell them you're showing them how much you love them. Even children find it difficult to be horrible to someone that's just told them that.

You should defend your spouse or ex-spouse against rudeness directed at him or her by your children (even if you secretly think it's deserved). The idea that both parents should be respected is a very important one to uphold at this time so don't let them play you off against each other; they may be the instigators but it will seriously unsettle them. If one of you loses their respect it's very likely that the other one will too (because you've broken down a huge boundary which makes it a much smaller step next time). Once children stop respecting their parents you have no control over their behaviour and you turn them into the anti-social monsters that think its OK to ignore and even abuse adults.

## Too clingy/childish

Some children will revert back to younger behaviour during this time. This is their way of telling you that they're scared and need you there for them. Give them lots of affection but spend time with them teaching them older, more independent skills and praise them for those. That way they see that they get the attention by being more adult and not by acting like a baby.

## Emotions

Your children will probably be aware or your emotional response to the divorce, good or bad, and that clearly can have an effect on them. One child told her counsellor, 'My mum is so happy now they've split up. I didn't know she was unhappy before. I don't really understand any of this.'

Research on people's emotional response to divorce shows a pattern of emotional highs and lows that most, but not all, go through. A few people I spoke to never experienced any lows and some, even where they'd instigated the divorce, never lost the feeling of sadness they felt about the end of the marriage. However usually, immediately after the divorce, people feel a sense of euphoria as they've freed themselves and see new possibilities opening up to them. This euphoria reaches a peak and they then enter a long downward phase, often prompted by being faced with some of the harsh realities of divorce, such as selling the house and having less money. During this downward phase divorcees are commonly very angry. Eventually this bottoms out and the divorcee feels at their lowest for a period. Hopefully this will improve as they start to rebuild their lives and move on from the pain of the divorce.

Knowing that you'll probably go through this cycle should help you understand what's happening to you and your ex. You should also use it to determine when you should attend mediation. Mediation will make your divorce easier, much less expensive and is consequently far preferable to expecting your lawyers to resolve your differences (see Chapter 4). However there are some stages in this emotional cycle when mediation will work and some when it's a waste of time. The best time has been found to be during the early euphoric phase, when you probably don't think you'll need it. After that you should only attempt it when you've both reached your lowest and the anger has begun to pass. Going for mediation during the angry phase is like trying to reason with a person when they've already lost their temper – you have to wait until the anger subsides.

You're probably well aware that the entire family is probably going to be very tense during this time. It's likely that on some occasions you'll overreact to quite minor offences, at the same time as your children are feeling most vulnerable and unloved. If this happens calmly and affectionately apologise to them as soon as you realise what's happened. Tell them that you're upset and were irritable and you shouldn't have been as angry as you were. Some parents worry about apologising to children, as they think it will lose them face. I found the opposite. Children learn from adults. If the adults in their lives carry on asserting they're right, even when they're clearly not, then that's what the children will do too. They will only learn the benefits of an apology, and the respect that can be regained from a sincere apology, when they've been on the receiving end of one. Apologising like this will also tell your children that they're not the only ones upset, that you're hurting too, which will stop them feeling alone with their grief or that grief and emotion is something to be ashamed of and should be buried.

## Grieving and moving on

Throughout this book I advocate hiding ill feeling between the parents, even when you're really angry with each other. This is to avoid putting your children in the position where they have split loyalties or feel that they should somehow get involved or make a judgement against one of their parents. If you didn't experience this as a child yourself the nearest comparison is when you have two best friends who fall out. You want to understand what's gone wrong but if they keep bitching about each other in front of you it's very uncomfortable. Should you defend the one who's not there? Does it mean that you can't ever talk favourably about the other one? Should you avoid mentioning the other altogether? Eventually you avoid both of your friends as you can no longer share things with them or talk openly with them about how you're feeling or about things that are on your mind for fear of raising the ill feeling or getting it directed at you. Is that how you want your children to feel about you?

But hiding ill feeling is not the same as hiding all emotion. It's very important that your children understand that you're not an automaton, that you have emotions and that you too are upset by the divorce. If you hide your emotions they may feel that you don't care. They may also take on board the message that emotions should be suppressed and that will make it difficult for them to get close to people in the future. Being upset and hurt is part of life; we all experience it and have to learn how to deal with it and move on. If you continue the arguments you had before the divorce, after the divorce (as so many people do) and blame all of life's ills on your ex you're teaching your children that pain never ends.

One of you may go through a period of extreme grief in the first months. Usually that's the person who didn't instigate the divorce. In that time they need space, possibly including time away from the children, and to see you as little as possible so that they have a chance to move on. If it's your ex who's the most upset by the separation, do allow them a period of mourning where they're given space and permission to grieve and recover. A friend of mine without children told me, 'We had an amicable divorce but the day my husband left our house five years ago was the last I saw him. I understand why: the best way to create distance between you is to not see each other at all.'

When you have children this is more difficult and it may affect your ex's ability to carry on life as normal and even to be a parent. Don't penalise them for that and recognise that they need to get angry with you and create a certain amount of distance from you. This can mean not seeing you or even speaking to you for a while. That makes sharing care difficult. You may find you need to take on more of the childcare yourself in these early days to help your ex through this. Typically the grieving period can last between 6 and 18 months.

### David's story:

My father left my mother after they had six children. She'd given her life to her family while he spent his time in an exciting job. I was so angry with him and, as I was the oldest, I felt responsible for my mum. The day he left she put her head on my shoulder and sobbed.

I struggled for years to make my own marriage work because I couldn't be responsible for doing to my wife and children what my father had done to Mum. But my wife was cold towards me and, probably because I was part of such a big family, I really need warmth and affection. I used to pray that my wife would have an affair or leave me so I wouldn't have to take on the guilt of leaving. But eventually I really couldn't stand it any longer and we agreed to part.

My own family were really supportive. Instead of blaming me they'd all expected it to happen sooner but that didn't stop me feeling overwhelmed with guilt. I love my children to bits, they're easily the most important thing in my life, but I couldn't bear to think about what I'd done to them so in the early months I scarcely saw them. Eventually it was my cold ex-wife who pointed out that I was letting them down and I found a way to deal with it.

The problem in grieving when you have children is that it may make them feel that they have no one to share their worries with. Another child told his counsellor, 'I can't tell Mummy how sad I am because she just cries all the time anyway. I don't know why but I think it might be because she has to look after me all by herself.' And another, 'I have tried to talk to Mum about how I feel about it all, but when I do, she just cries.'

Even if you did instigate the divorce you may well find that post-divorce life is much tougher than you were expecting.

### Eileen's story:

It was me that wanted the divorce; I was bored to the point of intense irritation with Billy, my husband. I thought he realised how I felt but he was devastated. At first I think he clung to the hope that I would change my mind. When I didn't he cried for months. Billy tried to stop seeing the boys for a while but that made me mad as I thought he was just trying to punish me for leaving him; but, looking back, I should have given him more space to grieve. The boys would spend the day with him and they'd phone me to say that Daddy had been crying for two hours what should they do? It was terrible.

Less than a year later he met someone else and a few months after that they got married. He's really happy now, much happier than he was with me. It makes it all worth it but I wish I'd handled that bit differently. I feel guilty about not giving him the space he needed.

I spoke to a number of children of divorced parents, now adults, whose parents separated and got back together many times. This is terribly unsettling for a child. It leaves them in a permanent state of terror and hope and doesn't allow anyone to recover and move on.

### Eddie's story:

My parents first split when I was about eight. I was really upset and desperately wanted them to get back together again. Just before Christmas my dad did come back and then left again a couple of months later. That happened most years from then on. I could never move on from the break-up, and neither could my mother, because each time we were moving on he would come back. It meant that I lived most of my childhood in that horrible first stage of parents splitting up. The few weeks he was with us I spent the whole time dreading him leaving again. As an adult it was clear to me what he was doing. He wanted to have all the freedoms of a single man but hated spending Christmas like that. I explained to my mother how selfish he was being and that she should stop being such a doormat. I can't believe she hadn't cottoned on to the fact it was always

Christmas when he came back. I'm really angry with my father for using us like that and constantly disrupting our lives through his selfishness.

## Gender and emotion

Surprisingly there still appears to be a huge gender difference in the way friendships can support people during times of crisis. Mike's story to me was very typical: 'I was close to a breakdown after my wife and I split but whenever I tried to talk about it to my male friends they would shift the subject immediately on to something more critical, like sport, and they also expected me to move on quickly. If they did support me at all it was simply to criticise my ex and because I still loved her I felt I had to defend her so they really were no help at all. I found women far more willing to listen to me and help me through it.'

If this gender difference is typical it may mean that your sons will need additional help during the divorce. They will be less likely to have female friends to turn to and, as they'll be less confident in their male identity, are more likely to stick to the male stereotype they see around them and avoid all mention of the stress they're under. The danger then is that burying worries like this often causes more stress which can come out as aggressive behaviour.

You may also be aware of the theory that if a woman tells you her worries she wants sympathy and if a man tells you his worries he wants you to help him find a solution. This is a stereotype but my experience is that generally it's true, but with either gender it's important to check. If you get it wrong you'll come across as unsympathetic or unhelpful. If your children do pour out their problems to you listen hard to determine what they actually want from you before you start to offer advice or sympathy. You should be able to quickly determine this from what they say and the way they say it. If not check their reaction to a small piece of advice. All solutions will be rejected without consideration if he or she wants sympathy and sympathy will be rejected in favour of discussing solutions to the problem if that's what he or she wants. If you keep getting it wrong and don't meet whichever need he or she has your child is less likely to open up to you in future.

## Articulating worries

Don't assume that your children will be affected badly. A child counsellor told me, 'Many parents now assume their children will need counselling but often that's not the case and assuming they will makes them take on the role of victim.' Instead listen to your child and their worries to see how they're handling things. Take them to a counsellor only if they show signs of having problems. This is dealt with in more detail in the final chapter.

Children all handle things differently and so different things will concern them. Sometimes their worries, though very real and important to the child, can be something so unexpected that you could never have predicted it. The same counsellor told me, 'An eight-year-old boy was referred to me because he was clearly very distressed by his parents' divorce. The parents had approached things amicably and he knew that there would be two houses and he would spend time with each of his parents in each house, but that seemed to really concern him. After a few hours of counselling I discovered that the cause of all his distress was his pet goldfish. The goldfish was important to him and, never having moved house, he didn't know that he would still be able to keep the fish.'

I've found that asking children if anything is wrong is usually useless. Education and discipline make children very good at telling adults what we want to hear, so you can't necessarily believe their reassurances that things are OK. I've looked at what my children do, far more than what they tell me, to gauge how they are emotionally. However one trick that's used in appraisals in corporate life can also be used at home. Choose a moment when you're all together (a family dinner is a good time) and ask your children to name two things that are going well in their lives or that they're proud of and the two things that worry them most. Everyone in the family can take part but use your turn to talk about things that have an impact on your children too, rather than increasing their worries about things that they don't need to know about, alternatively think of things that will make them laugh and relieve any tension that your children feel. Demonstrate to your children that you too have recognised that you're going to have to work hard on some things, for example, 'I'm worried that I'm not going to be able to spend enough time with my children now I have to work longer hours.' When talking of the things you're proud of try to say something about how proud you are of your children. Make them honest recognitions of what they're good at. Get everyone to write down their worries and put them into a 'proud' box and a 'worry' box. Each person then draws one issue from each hat and says them out loud. The family can then all discuss the issues together without anyone feeling particularly exposed. So long as you can get past it feeling a little silly to begin with, it does get the conversation going.

One thing you probably already realise as a parent is that children's emotions can be very fickle. They can be devastated about something one minute and a few minutes later have completely forgotten about it. That means you can't assume that what's upset them yesterday is even on their radar today and it's important to keep things in perspective. I was recently feeling very low because Gabriella's boyfriend had dumped her. She was devastated and, as her mother, I couldn't feel happy while she was suffering so much. I felt pretty daft when I discovered that, far from still grieving like I was, she was actually happily seeing a new boy. As she explained, her ex was 'ancient' history, even if it was less than a week later.

## The day

How you handle the day you and your spouse start to live separately will partly depend on how old your children are. If they're very young it's a good idea for them to spend the day with a much-loved friend or relative who understands the situation. Older children may want to be part of things and get involved. That's fine if you're both happy with them being there and things aren't going to be too tense.

It's very important that one of you doesn't just disappear. I spoke to many adults who'd experienced this as children and all of them confessed that they spent their lives terrified that the people they love will one day just disappear from their lives. It's better instead if the parent who will not be with the children that night helps them settle into their new home and shows an interest in their new bedroom, perhaps even offering to help get things right for them. This will establish the idea that you're still there to help and support them, wherever they are.

When things are unpacked and everyone is settled try and have a meal together – even if it's a takeaway – as a family for possibly the last time. When one of you leaves give the children an affectionate hug and make sure they know exactly when you'll see them again; it's a good idea if that's very soon, perhaps take them to school in the morning so that this feels less of a big deal. As soon as possible get their bedrooms set up in their other home so that the children can quickly visualise what their new life will be like as the reality will stop them worrying about the details.

In my case we sold our house with no problems but my new place was ready several weeks before my ex's, so he stayed in 'my' house for a few weeks. During that time I helped him decorate the girls' bedrooms and we bought new furniture which seriously confused the salesman (it was worth doing it just for that – 'Yes, I'm his wife, but I won't be living there, so he can have the leather monstrosity of a sofa and it really doesn't bother me at all.'). That was a very strange time and I think we both see the day we sold the family home as the day we really separated. When the removal men had picked up all our stuff we had time for lunch in the pub. Every single song that came on the jukebox was about breaking up and how hard it was to do. After about the tenth song we both couldn't help laughing and that relieved some of the tension.

The day that my ex-husband's place was ready the men got everything into the van and he shouted 'Bye, then' to the girls and to me. Stephanie and I gave him a hug and Gabriella just shouted 'Bye!' from her room. It was only later that she realised that with her casual goodbye, she'd just said farewell to normal family life.

We did fulfil one last promise to the children and that was to take them to Disneyland six months after we separated. Somehow we slipped back into 'normal' family life during that holiday which made the separation at the end of it even more strange and painful, as if we were separating all over again. I'm not sure I would recommend it; I think it can send out confusing messages to children, but it did mean that our actual separation was done in many stages: the house being sold, my ex moving out and then the holiday; so the sudden shock of their dad not being around was not something they had to go through.

The above may all seem a bit too friendly but we both recognised that the moment we stopped being a couple our relationship was no longer about us and how we felt; everything between us was over and what was left was the fact that we were parents of children we both adored and wanted to shield from hurt. Our interactions with each other were about doing what was best for them; not about our arguments, as they were no longer relevant. Mundane things, like shopping for furniture, reassured them that we would both be there for them as united parents, but if you can't do that without sniping at each other it will have a negative rather than positive impact on your children.

## Leaving for a new relationship

If you're leaving your marriage for a new relationship it's important to leave a gap of at least six months between leaving your spouse and introducing (and moving in with) your new partner. There are three reasons for doing that. Dating when you're free is different to when you're married and people often find that the new relationship doesn't work out.

It's very disruptive for your children to get used to a new person and for them to then leave as suddenly. Secondly, because you've sacrificed so much, including your children's happiness, you'll find there's huge pressure on the new relationship to succeed. Giving yourself a breathing period will allow for the relationship to be tested without that additional pressure. Lastly it will give your children a chance to get used to their parents being apart before they're introduced to someone else and this will make it less likely they'll resent your new partner.

When you do move in with your new partner it is far better for a new home to be found than for one of you to move in with the other. If you don't the adult and children who lived there first will always feel it's their home, whoever's name is on the rental agreement or mortgage, and your children will feel like the unwanted extras; Cinderella to the ugly sisters. It's a hassle; it'll cost you money, but in terms of helping children feel like they belong to the family it will make a huge difference.

If you can't start afresh in a new home arrange it so that your children move in with you before your new partner and any stepchildren come home (like they do on TV's *Wife Swap*). This will reduce the feeling that they're guests in someone else's home while they settle in. Make sure that there is room for them, for example, clear drawers, wardrobe space and shelf space before they arrive. If possible make sure they have their own rooms. Go overboard with the welcome and focus the first few nights around them. Emphasise that this is their home as well now.

# Other people

You may find that your children see a lot of one or more of their friends. Commonly this time with their friends is 'escape time' where they can hide for a few hours from the emotional fallout from the divorce. They don't have to worry whether these friends are about to cry or are upset about something one of you has done or not done and they don't have to be careful about what they say in case it upsets you. There is no feeling that they should be taking sides or protecting one of you from the other; they can be a carefree child again. Of course these friends may also be their confidant and provide your child with someone to download all their emotions to; which may include being very critical of you and what you're doing. Try not to feel threatened by it; we all need someone like this and children are no different. It's far better that your children have a good moan about you to a friend than they internalise it and feel alone with their anger and terror. If left the problems will feel magnified to them and are far more likely to cause long-term harm.

With relatives, ensure that they understand the rules of the divorce and don't try and turn the children away from your ex. If your children are close to one or more of your relatives encourage them to spend a little more time with them. These trusted adults are likely to be able to supply both security and someone to confide in. The world seems less unstable if you have a steady object to look at. Grandparents can often supply exactly that.

Teenagers sometimes try to substitute the warmth and security that they no longer find at home with a sexual relationship. Don't make the mistake of assuming your child won't. Make sure you keep in touch with what's happening in their lives and whether they need sex education before they either hurt themselves further, when they're emotionally vulnerable, or make a mistake that messes up their lives. If they do you'll need to be there to pick up the pieces.

Teachers and other professionals do not normally have the time to provide active support for your children. However sometimes children will confide in a teacher so, particularly if your children are young, it's worth making sure they know that your child will be going through a difficult time.

## Sarah's story:

I'm a teaching assistant and it's really obvious when children are experiencing problems at home. I remember one case particularly well because this little boy changed so dramatically and so suddenly. He went from being a lovely, well-mannered child to this horror that was causing real problems in class and it was clear to us that he was really unhappy.

We called his mother in and asked her if there were any problems at home that could have unsettled her son. She told us she couldn't think what it was and went through a few minor incidents; eventually she mentioned almost in passing that she and the boy's father were separating but added, 'Obviously that's not going to affect him as he's only four.' We couldn't believe that this silly woman didn't realise that children pick up on these things and how badly it often affects them. This poor child was worrying about losing his father and his whole life being disrupted and they hadn't thought to even talk to him about it and assumed that it wouldn't bother him!

As a parent, you're not their whole world, nor should you wish to be. The older your children are the more important other people will be in their lives. A school-age child should spend far more time with their friends than they do with you. These friends, relations and even teachers will all affect how your children handle your divorce. You should encourage this.

# Chapter 3

---

## Practical Arrangements

---

- How to decide what to do with the children
- Excuses
- Things to consider
- Dealing with crisis situations

Children, like the rest of us, are usually most afraid of the unknown. Once you tell them that you're separating they'll probably start to worry about what will happen to them, where they'll live, whether they'll still be loved and 101 other things you won't even anticipate. They'll probably keep worrying until you prove to them that life will go on and things will be all right but the only way you'll convince them of that is when they see it for themselves by experiencing their new life. You therefore need to agree something as quickly as possible and then stick to that routine.

# How to decide what to do with the children

The practical arrangements for your children should take into account what suits them and not just what's convenient for the parents or who has more 'right' to the children. That's irrelevant. Parents do not have a moral 'right' to their children: children have a moral right to their parents – *both* their parents. Nor should the arrangements be affected by the disputes between the two or you or by stereotypes of which gender takes care of what.

It's important that when you divorce you don't carry over the bitterness and accompanying arguments into your post-divorce life. A child counsellor told me, 'Women are often so bitter towards their ex-husbands that they will battle really hard to get them out of their lives, which includes stopping them from having any contact with their children. If they succeed in that they'll see it as a huge victory without recognising the damage they're doing to their children and the problems they're storing up for themselves. Other mothers will manipulate their children into not wanting to see their fathers. For example, "Do you really want to go and see your father instead of coming shopping with me? Of course it's entirely up to you; his new girlfriend's going to be there, the one you don't like, and he sounded in a bad mood but of course I wouldn't stop you. It's entirely your decision."'

To best serve your children's long-term happiness, it was very obvious from everyone I spoke to that you should work to ensure that your children are able to enjoy the maximum amount of quality time at home with each of their parents. If you make it difficult for your partner to have a relationship with their children then you're denying your children one of their most important human rights and one day they'll judge you for that. Similarly, and just as often ignored, it's important that they are able to form and maintain friendships and activities outside the home.

## The role of fathers

Many people believe that we live in an equal society but most still demonstrate remarkably old-fashioned views when it comes to divorce and children. It's still common for women to assume that they have more right to their children based on their primary care role and for men not to realise that their children are just as much their responsibility. Similarly some men still feel ownership of their offspring in a way that suggests that the children are simply a recreation of them and therefore represent their future 'dynasty', with little to do with the mother other than as a servant of the children.

I'm shocked by the statistic from the National Association of Child Contact Centres (NACC) that suggests that around half of fathers are believed to lose all contact with their children within two years of divorce. I asked a number of fathers who are part of that statistic why, and they nearly all gave me the same response: their ex-wife had made it too difficult and too distressing to see the children so they'd come to the conclusion that it was better for everyone if they stopped trying.

Rather than just be appalled by this, it's useful to examine why. Women are still discriminated against at work and men are discriminated against when it comes to divorce and access to children. The two are related. Employers are more prejudiced against mothers with young children than any other group, including the disabled. I can see why. They're the group most likely to have to take time off without warning to care for their children when they're sick, for example, or when care arrangements break down, as they often do. This is very tough on women, particularly if the father always assumes that their job is too important to share that burden, and their wife's career will suffer as a result. But the effect on fathers can be even more devastating. If you're a father who behaves like that you're effectively saying to your wife that her role is to look after the children and yours is to provide for them. You may have been happy with that while you were married but think what it means now you're getting divorced. If her role is to care for the children, where does that leave you in their lives except as the provider of maintenance? You shouldn't be too surprised if your wife expects you to continue in the same role as you assumed in the past.

If you want your children to live with you some of the time after you're divorced, then take on some of that responsibility now. The law is against you, the statistics are horrifying, so do what you can to demonstrate clearly that you're both capable of looking after your children and are committed to them. Also make sure that your children accept you as a carer. Next time your children are ill or some other emergency requires a parent at home, make sure it's you that takes time off work and see how your employer reacts. If you want to take on a full parenting role after the divorce you can't expect your ex to be the one fitting her life around the children when you have care of them.

### Ian's story:

I always regarded myself as a great dad. My wife's friends even told her how lucky she was and I was pretty smug about it. I made that judgement based on the fact that I played with the children and would read to them, but of course that's the easy bit of being a parent. When we got divorced we arranged things so that I had the children every other weekend and two days during the week. The first time I had them all my self-congratulatory smugness evaporated. I'd never been alone with my children before and hadn't realised what that meant. My wife had even taken them shopping with her on a Saturday when we were married so that I wasn't left alone with them. My sons, who played with me so happily before, were so unused to me caring for them without their mother to step in when they needed her that they cried most of the time they were with me and I had no idea how to do the basics for them or what going outside the home actually meant in terms of equipment and safety. Playing with children for half an hour does not prepare you for hands-on parenting.

## Excuses

There are numerous reasons why people feel that their children should spend all or the majority of time with them after the divorce, with their ex only getting the occasional 'access' visits. A few of these are valid; most of them are outrageous. If you believe your children should spend most or the majority of their time with you, check your reasons against the list below and ask yourself some tough questions to make sure you get it right. Do you want to risk losing your children altogether? If your reason for denying your ex-spouse access to the children is for a selfish motive, your children will eventually, however much propaganda you use, see that you robbed them of one of their parents. They'll find it very difficult to forgive you for that. I've spoken to many adults who have bitter relationships with their mother (and sometimes father) because they were used by their mother or father like this. And even before then you're setting yourself up for a tough life as a single parent.

The excuses are commonly one or a combination of the following:

## He or she cheated on us

No, your spouse didn't; he or she cheated on *you*. The sexual and emotional fidelity obligation doesn't include children. If your partner is adulterous it makes them a selfish and inconsiderate spouse that has caused upset to the family, but it doesn't stop them being a good parent in the future, unless you confuse the two.

## He or she walked out on us

The issue of people walking out on their children is dealt with later in this chapter under the heading 'Dealing with crisis situations'. However in most cases it's the spouse that the partner walked out on, and if you think you'll need to fight them for the children then that is very obviously the case.

## He or she never spends any time with the children anyway/is disinterested in them

If that's true your job, for the sake of your children, is to encourage your ex and make sure that, if he or she changes their minds, the door is open for them to resume their role as a parent. However I've heard many women say this when in fact they mean that Dad has been working so hard to fulfil his historic role as provider he's been pushed out. If your ex is really disinterested in the children then it's unlikely that they'll ask for custody, and if they do as part of their battle with you, they'll soon lose interest again. If they don't you've misjudged them.

### Eric's story:

Divorce was easy, as we both wanted it; dividing up the assets was easy because I was happy for her to take what she needed and she quickly moved in with a new man. But we've had huge problems over the children. My ex-wife really didn't think I had the right to a role in my children's lives any more and me wanting one was just me 'being difficult'. I think she wanted her new partner to be their 'dad', although she denied it.

I'd worked long hours before the separation, often coming home after the children were in bed. Like many men, I'd fallen into the traditional role of provider as soon as I became a father; as she had as a mother. She wanted to stay at home and, with the family reduced to one income, I needed to get promoted as soon as possible. Why should that be used as proof that I loved my children less than she did? I wish I'd worked less and told her we couldn't afford for her to stay at home. Then she couldn't have used my efforts to support my family as evidence that I wasn't interested in them. It now costs me £400 in lawyers' letters just so I can be 'allowed' to collect my own children from school.

## I don't want my children to see his or her new partner

However tough it is you have to accept that your children will have a new family of step-relations. The easier you make it for them to adapt to that the happier they'll be. Your battle with your ex and the person he or she left you for has to be kept out of this. If you think you have the moral right to stop your children seeing the new partner then you clearly believe you have more rights over your children than your spouse. You don't.

## He or she broke up the family

You and your spouse broke up the family by not being what the other needed any more.

## I want to punish my ex and the only weapon I have is to deny them access to their children

Great that you can be so honest with yourself but it's a weapon that will explode in your face. You'll harm yourself just as much as you harm your ex and you'll harm the children most of all. Would you do your children physical injury if you thought it would upset your ex? Of course not, so why do you think it's OK to do them serious emotional harm for that same reason?

### Eleanor's story:

We had the 'perfect' life. We had lots of money, two lovely little boys and my husband appeared to dote on me and his family: he seemed to find it difficult to be apart from us even for a day. He appeared proud of his family to the point of obsession.

Then one day, after he'd been a bit off with me for a few weeks, I asked if something was wrong and my husband told me he didn't love me any more and wanted a break. He told me that I was a wonderful person, that it was the biggest gamble of his life but he needed to spend time away from me (I've since found out that this is a pretty standard speech for this situation). It felt like I'd gone from being worshipped to being unwanted overnight; it was a horrible shock. He didn't tell me at the time, but I found out later, that there was another woman and shortly after he moved in with her.

It's very tempting but I refuse to pass on my anger and hurt to my children. My father left my mother when I was 11 and she ruined my teenage years with her bitterness and there's no way I want that for my boys. I've therefore limited what I've told them and gone out of my way to encourage them to be on good terms with their father. This week has been the most testing one so far, as my ex is two weeks late with the maintenance payments. I had a great job before I had children but he urged me to give it up and now I'm reliant on him. I know that many people would urge me not to let him see the boys until he's given me the money he owes me; we're having to go without while he and his new family have a very comfortable lifestyle. But as tempting as that is, I know, from my own experience, that it would hurt my children so I won't do it.

## My lawyer says that if I win an 'unreasonable behaviour' divorce I could get full access with only occasional custody visits

So what? Do you want to get all you can out of this divorce in the short term or do you want to ensure you have happy, emotionally stable children?

## He or she is always late/unreliable just to annoy me

Quietly point it out, away from the ears of the children and in a constructive way rather than as opener to an argument. If it doesn't actually cause any problems and is just irritating then try to bite your tongue and let it go. If they're really doing it to annoy you then you'll be taking that incentive away from them. Don't be tempted to repay them by being late yourself. Instead, if the offence continues, pretty well assume they'll be late and get on with other things until they arrive so that everyone stays calm and relaxed. Be approximate when you tell the children what time they're being picked up, 'Daddy said he'd be here between two and four.'

If your ex makes a habit of not turning up at all make sure he or she understands the upset it causes the children and ask them to ensure they phone and tell the children if there are any reasons why they're unable to make it. Some people would rather let people assume they're not coming than face having to speak to someone and hear the disappointment or annoyance first-hand. It's rude and cowardly, particularly where children are involved, but eventually everyone, including the children, will learn not to rely on them and be pleasantly surprised when they do turn up. Don't assume that they're getting away with this behaviour; your children will make their own mental notes without you poisoning the air with your anger.

## He (usually he) has no idea how to look after children – men aren't able to look after young children

In life there are few things we're good at without some practice and even then some of us are better than others. I've yet to meet a man who, with practice, isn't just as good a parent as the average woman. Men may parent slightly differently to women but I've seen them master everything from bottle feeding a baby with projectile vomiting while looking after a toddler with a tantrum to making Roman-style outfits at midnight. In my experience they're not much good with ribbons and bows, though, but hardly a reason for a child not to see their daddy. If the children are very young to begin with you may need to help, or find someone else to teach them the basics, but in my experience people pick it up very quickly. They may also need to be returned to you at night if you're their only attachment figure (see 'The options' below).

## He or she is a bad parent

Who says so? Attend mediation to see what a disinterested third party thinks. You can't rely on the judgement of your friends as they hear your side of the story and are there to support you, so are not unbiased. Unless there are issues of abuse or other forms of danger then it's not your call. There are lots of people I think are bad parents but it doesn't give me the right to take their children away from them (I'm sure they think the same of some of my parenting skills).

### Simon's story:

My wife walked out on me to be with another man and left me with our four children who were all under five at the time. It was a terrible struggle; I had to give up my job and become a full-time dad. Two years later my ex-wife reappeared and demanded custody of the children and I quickly agreed that we should share care. My youngest, a girl, didn't want to know her mother to begin with so I had to work hard to get the relationship going again. Some of my friends were surprised and even critical that I let my ex-wife back into their lives but she's their mother, nothing she'd done changed that, and the only reason to keep the children to myself would have been to punish her, which is pretty daft. Her coming back into the children's lives was good for everyone, including me, as at last I had a chance of having a semblance of a life again. When people fight over custody they have no idea how hard bringing up children without the support of a partner is going to be.

## He or she only wants the children so that they don't have to pay child support

Are you sure, or is that what you're telling yourself? If it's true then they're in for a shock as support payments don't usually actually cover the true cost of children, particularly childcare and the pressure on your working life, so they're likely to lose money and soon want you to have the children back.

## He or she is abusive

If that means they're a stricter parent than you are then it's irrelevant. However if your partner is violent, to you or the children, then clearly it does more harm than good keeping them in your lives. You should, if possible, get it established in court, while the evidence is available, so that you reduce the risk of the law giving your ex access again. This is one occasion where I would encourage you to use a lawyer. This subject is dealt with in more detail below: 'Dealing with crisis situations'.

## He or she is an addict

If the addiction is not being treated then the children do need to be removed from the parent's care. However if there are times of the day when the parent is sober then supervised visits so that the children can keep some relationship going should be possible. Addiction does not include the occasional recreational use of drugs or alcohol. However morally offensive you find it, it is now so common that nearly half of children would need to be taken away from their parents.

## It's best for the children that they're not disrupted and spend all their time with me

Your children want to feel loved by both their parents. If they say otherwise it's usually because you've either made them feel that they have to say that out of loyalty to you or because you've made spending time with your ex difficult for them in some way (and there are lots of ways you can do that). You should make the time they spend with their other parent as easy and happy as you can.

If moving between homes is disruptive have a look why and if there are ways to ease it. If your ex is making things uncomfortable for them at his or her place see if you can negotiate some changes.

## The children don't want to see him/her

This is a difficult issue. You should listen to your children and act in their best interests but is their immediate anger or upset really something that should be allowed to destroy their whole relationship with one of their parents? When they look back on their childhood the absence of a father or a mother from their lives is likely to be a source of sadness, long after they remember the detail of the reasons and events that led to it. I think you need to examine very carefully why the child is so against one of you. Children will have torn loyalties; you need to help them overcome that by making it clear that you would like to see them spend time with your ex.

Has your ex made them uncomfortable or behaved badly in some way towards them? You're in a much better position than your ex to understand your child's reluctance and then help your ex understand the reasons behind this. I know that can be very difficult as the most common reaction to this feedback is that you're poisoning their minds in some way. You therefore need to be helpful rather than accusatory. For example, 'Jack is finding it difficult to get on with his stepbrothers and doesn't feel part of your new family yet' is likely to be more useful than, 'Jack doesn't like staying with you.' 'Jack hates you' is not worth saying but, 'Jack is feeling protective towards me and is still angry with you for leaving. I think we may need to sit down together again and explain things' might help the situation. To check on how threatening what you're saying is (and therefore the likely reaction of your ex) turn it round and think how you'd feel if your ex said it to you.

## Things to consider

Your aim is to find a way for your children to be able to hang out in a natural comfortable way with both their parents in their new homes, just like they do now. That means time to slob out together, not short tense visits where everyone feels like they have to be on their best behaviour. You want them to continue to feel they have two parents, not one parent and a relative they see occasionally.

If the children are very young (under five) you need to keep in mind that they need a consistent 'attachment' figure. This is usually the mother. Young children should not be taken away from the attachment figure for long periods of time and he or she should always be on hand in case of illness or other stress. In rare cases where the father or other parent has had a very active role, then each of the parents may be able to act in that role. I believe my own marriage was one example of that. I worked part-time, my ex worked shifts. He had sole care of the children nearly as much as I did and he was a great dad, so they did not show a preference. The time to test this is when they're ill. If they're just as happy being comforted by either one of you and don't call out for the other, then you can assume that you can each act as the attachment figure.

You should try to organise things to suit their lives and the things that are important to them. If, for example, they love football try to ensure that they can continue playing every week and not have to let the team down every month because they're with a different parent. These activities and friends form an important part of their development that you shouldn't ignore just because it makes things difficult for you. Of all the things you do to help your children through your divorce this is probably the one that will have the most impact on their ability to lead a normal happy childhood.

You should also try to set things up so that they'll work even when new partners come on to the scene. You may be in the 'never again' territory at the moment but the right pair of twinkling eyes can throw the most determined single divorcees back down the aisle and you don't want to have to disrupt your children's lives at that point any more than you have to.

Whatever option you go for you should try to divide your

children's time with each of you evenly, but you may need to make allowances for your pattern of work, the age of the children and any practical issues. If the children are very young it may be better for them to return to the attachment figure every night. Teenagers, by contrast, will be very happy staying with one parent for a block of time, upsetting them and then moving into a new household without having to live in the atmosphere that they just created!

The idea of living in two homes may sound disruptive but children adapt to it remarkably well. If the children express some doubt reassure them that it's very much like being the child of an international jet-setter who also live in different homes, only with this arrangement they can still nip back to collect stuff if they forget it.

Where one of you has taken on the role of primary carer the other should not then go out and create a 'bachelor' pad at their place. If you're to have significant chunks of time with your children you need to ensure that, as far as you can within your resources, your place is somewhere that they feel comfortable. You'll recall that in the first chapter I advised that children need access to age-appropriate toys and surroundings. Check that you have that. Do your children have outside space to play safely? Do you have toys to keep them interested and occupied or do you expect them to bring things with them? When they visit do you have other guests there? Is that really necessary? Do these guests know how to behave around children? Do your children feel safe at your place? Don't assume, find out. They'll probably tell you what you want to hear so you need to ask open-ended questions. It's unlikely they'll want to share you with an assortment of strangers, particularly if they're under the influence of alcohol or drugs. It sounds obvious but, from the people I've spoken to, apparently it isn't. I know one man who had to share one of his parent's homes with huge quantities of hard drugs and an assortment of famous punk musicians from the 1970s when he was five years old. He now suffers from panic attacks and other psychological issues. You may think that the party lifestyle is exciting and stimulating; a young child will not have the social skills to deal with it and will find it uncomfortable at best and possibly even terrifying.

Children should believe that their parents are 'on hand' when they need them. In both homes they should feel like they're at home and not a guest which means they need to have a bed and their own stuff at both addresses. It also means they should be treated as part of the family and not someone there temporarily on sufferance.

## The ideal

The solution that fits all the above requirements and makes life easiest for everyone is for you and your ex to find new homes just a few minutes away from each other. By living close I don't mean you should both live in the same street; you don't want to be able to see the comings and goings in your ex's house. Living close means that it doesn't matter which home they're in they can still go to football, tiddly-wink lessons (or whatever else they do) and see the same friends. They can also easily see the other parent when they want to, particularly if they have some exciting news, want to show you their latest artwork or simply want a cuddle and a chat. You're both still accessible when they need you and that makes a huge difference to children emotionally. It also means that they can attend the same school whichever parent they live with, and so it is one of the only solutions that makes it practical for children to live a similar amount of time with each parent in a natural way.

This is also the easiest solution for most parents. The children are never too far away from you, which I find reassuring, as it means I can be on hand for crises and triumphs. In addition, neither of you has to use up your entire weekends chauffeuring your children between activities and friends some distance away because that's where your ex lives. Most people underestimate the disruption this causes to their lives until they're experiencing it.

I tried living a little further away from my ex for a short while. It was a huge mistake and immediately caused problems even though we were still close enough for the girls to stay at the same schools. Seeing their friends became a challenge (it involved them travelling further than I wanted them to at odd hours) and they were in danger of being left out of the 'groups' they valued so highly. Accidentally leaving something at one house became an hour-long round trip (sometimes followed immediately by another one) and getting them to weekend activities became such a chore that they were dropped. It really highlighted how much easier we'd made things by living close so I moved back.

Genny, a mother of three children now grown up, agrees, 'My ex-husband lived for a couple of years just ten minutes away but then moved to more than an hour's drive away. Life was so much simpler for the children when he lived down the road. They used to see him all the time and he could help out with some of the day-to-day stuff. As soon as he moved away it became a real chore for them to go and see him. In effect it meant giving up most of a weekend and they had other things they wanted to do. I made the effort for a while but now they're older and can drive I leave it up to them to see their father. The visits have reduced to a couple of times a year and he's become more like a distant relative to them than a father.'

Most of the people I've suggested the above to have protested that they don't want to risk bumping into their ex all the time. I can understand that, and would find it uncomfortable myself, but I've lived most of the last six years less than five minutes walk from my ex and have never, not even once, bumped into either him or his new wife.

One variation to this, which is rare but works for some, is if the parents themselves swap homes instead of the children but I can't see that working well when you have new partners and it does take a lot of trust.

## Living at a distance

There are reasons why living close might not be possible, such as other children being part of the equation or work commitments making it difficult, but do think these through before you make any assumptions as the alternatives will make life much more difficult, for everyone.

If you're living so far away that it's not possible for the children to attend the same school from both homes it immediately limits the way the children's time can be divided between you. This means you'll need to find an arrangement where one of you has them during school time and the rest of the time is divided up. This causes a number of problems that you'll need to work around:

- How can your children be part of a sports team (or other activity) if they spend chunks of their time in a different area? Effectively they'll need a 'taxi' service which can use up the whole of your weekends and is a real pain, particularly if you have many children as you'll find you have no time to relax.

- How can your children be part of their gang of friends if their friends can never remember whose house they're at? You'll need to be the one making sure this happens. School-age children should be with their friends more than they're with you so don't underestimate this issue.

- How can you both be accessible by your children whenever they need you?

## 'Sunday afternoon' access visits and the variants

Go to any zoo and most fast-food restaurants on a Sunday and you'll see sad little scenes of fathers with their children trying to find things to say to each other. I shudder whenever I see them. These arrangements are common but cause so many problems that they often result in the end of contact between the children and parents involved. They also result in child counsellors having to sort out emotionally distraught children. One counsellor gave me an insight into the cause of the problems that they create so, if you're stuck with this arrangement, you can anticipate and avoid some of the issues.

- The reluctant attitude of the other parent (usually the mother) causing anxiety for the child. You should avoid making your child feel that they're missing out on something, being disloyal to you by going or in any way make the visit anything other than exciting.

Talk about it in an encouraging positive way; 'I bet you're looking forward to seeing Dad. I know he's really looking forward to seeing you.' You want your children to feel that they can happily share this part of their lives with you, not bottle it up as a shameful secret. I know that will probably be difficult for you to begin with.

- The child is required to fit in with the 'Sunday' parent's lifestyle/activity/company, etc, with little opportunity for the child to spend time with the parent without siblings. If you only see your child on a Sunday, and spend the rest of your time with your new family, your child should be your number one priority during their visit and your time together should be special. That doesn't mean you have to go out or do anything expensive, just that you devote time to them and don't, as so often seems to be the case, leave it to your new partner to take care of the child while you get on with reading the papers, doing the gardening and whatever else you do. Instead sit down with them and find out what's going on in their lives, listen to their triumphs and their worries. Take them away from the strangers that are your new family and let them have the time they miss with you the rest of the week. Eventually they may enjoy time with your new family but do remember they come to see you, not them. This last point is dealt with in much more detail in Chapter 6.

- The emotional state of the 'Sunday' parent. The parent can be very emotional when seeing their children, especially if there is a custody / access struggle going on. It is down to the two of you, as parents, to avoid lumbering your child with the bitterness you feel against each other, particularly at this precious time. Try to think of something friendly and positive to say to each other in the brief handover period. If you're feeling really bitter it's probably best to focus the conversation on the child. 'Jack's got a gold star in English didn't you, Jack?'

- Arrangements are 'set' for access without flexibility, which means your children may miss friends' parties, sports matches, outings and other important things in their lives. A typical comment from a child on this; 'I hate going to Dad's. He lives miles away from all my mates. It's really boring going there.' Another told her counsellor, 'I live with my gran and I have to go to mum's one weekend, and dad's the other. I really want to stay at gran's where I have all my stuff but I am only there during the week.' In each case the child's need to have a home where they can carry on the important business of being a child is ignored. Many parents have complained to me how things such as children's parties get in the way of their weekends with the children. To me that problem is looked at back to front and these parents aren't recognising how important those parties are.

The other issues lie around the fact that so many of these visits involve 'doing' something. This can either be because the parent doesn't have accommodation that's suitable for the children (they've been left in a bedsit or shared house while the other parent has the family home) or they think that's how to make the visit special. The visit should not be seen as a competition with the rest of a child's life eg, 'Don't you have a better time with me than your mum?' That just creates tension and an honest (but precociously articulate) answer from the child would be: 'No, because you want me to be disloyal to the mother I love and your question suggests that you feel you have to prove that you're better than she is. I don't want to feel torn between the two of you.' Similarly don't feel you always have to do something and then put the burden of what to do on the child. If you do go out it's far better for that to be the two of you (and their other brothers and sisters) than bringing your new partner or step-siblings until it's evident that they are close to their new stepfamily. If you have more than one child find time to have one-to-one time with each of your children.

## Changing the arrangements

If one of you is due to have the children on a certain day then finds they can't they retain responsibility for finding a baby-sitter; they should not assume that the other one steps in (although it makes sense for both of you to help each other out as much as is feasible).

It's often difficult to fit your holiday into the time when you have your children. Be flexible with each other to allow for this but make sure you warn your ex in plenty of time. Don't assume that it will be all right; they may well have organised something themselves.

As children get older their needs, emotional and practical, change. You'll also find that your own life will change, you may have a new partner who has children; those children may live in a different area. All this means that you need to review the arrangements regularly both with your ex and with the children to see if they're working and to see if they could be improved. The older the children are the more you need to take their wishes and needs into consideration.

# Dealing with crisis situations

The practical arrangements described above will not be relevant if you've separated without warning, have broken off all contact with each other and are now trying to deal with the aftermath. The reasons for this sudden separation will obviously affect how you handle things.

## Physical abuse

If you've left because you fear for your safety you're likely to need help (professional and from friends and family) to overcome the huge emotional and practical problems you're going to face. Don't feel guilty about asking for it. Consider how you'd feel if one of your family or friends were in this situation; you'd probably be offended if they didn't come to you for help, particularly where there are children involved.

You may have trouble convincing your children that it was necessary to leave. This happens even when the children have witnessed, or even been subject to, the abuse. Children are more likely to believe it when someone says that they won't do it again and they will fear change more than their unhappy reality. They won't know, like you do, that this is not normal and that life can and should be better. You'll need to explain that the behaviour was wrong and dangerous.

However I would still limit criticism of your ex as much as you can. This person is still part of them, criticising him or her will still hurt.

If your ex is likely to try to find you to continue the abuse, seek help from the courts, and note the details and dates of any threats, so that you can you use these to get an injunction if necessary.

This is one of the few examples where I would not encourage you to try to share the parenting of your children with your ex, so you'll need to read the rest of this book with that in mind. See Chapter 5 and the section on 'Coping with sole custody', for more advice on handling this type of situation.

## They walked out

It's very common for people to put their spouse and children into one mental compartment which they label 'family'. Some people take this attitude to the extreme so that when the marriage goes wrong for them, or when they fall in love with someone else, they walk out on the whole family to begin a new life without a backward glance. Men used to be the worse culprits of this behaviour but there are many cases now where women have done it too. It's obviously devastating for everyone. As the spouse you'll have to deal with a loss that is, in many ways, more devastating than your partner dying. However, for your children this is the worst type of betrayal: if one parent can abandon them like that what is there to stop the other one doing the same? Despite your grief, for your children's sake and however bitter you rightly feel, you should try to make your ex realise that he or she continues to have a responsibility for your children and that it is quite separate from their relationship with you. Make seeing his or her children as easy as possible, by ensuring, for example, that the changeover can happen without you being there.

There are other reasons for people disappearing from their life that have little if anything to do with the family they leave. The most common is mental illness which comes in many forms (including addiction) and is the most likely explanation if you don't believe that there is another person involved. This is dealt with separately below.

Your efforts to keep your ex in your children's lives might not pay off straight away. Ensure that he or she is updated on any changes to your contact details and get the children to send birthday and Christmas cards for around two years. This might seem to be dragging things out but if you read interviews with these parents few consciously meant to block their families out of their lives. It usually started with a crisis, in anger, in the first rush of love under someone else's influence or some other mental disturbance. They then try to turn their back on their family as a way of blocking out pain, or because they thought it was the only way of moving on from a situation they couldn't cope with. Many of these people come to bitterly regret what they've done but feel it's too late to go back to their families; they feel so bad about it that they don't believe they've got that right or will be accepted again.

I can understand the victims of this behaviour believing that they and their children are much better off without a person who can be so selfish and cause so much pain. But your children won't be. They may be angry when they see the parent again, they may say that they hate them, but just knowing that their parent wants them again will take a huge emotional burden off their shoulders. For their sake you therefore need to give your ex every chance to make it up to his or her children and do what you can to help rebuild the relationship. That includes being very careful how you explain the behaviour.

However there does come a point where you need to help your children accept that the parent is unlikely to re-enter their lives.

### Louise's story:

I remember my father as a lovely warm man who always got on well with all my friends. When I was 12 this same man waited until my sister and I were at school, and my mother was at work, packed all his stuff and left it in the hall. When we got home he told my mother he didn't love her any more, picked up his bags and left. At the time he claimed there was no one else involved, but not long afterwards he moved in with another woman and shortly after that he asked me to be his bridesmaid at his wedding. I refused and have had no relationship with him from the day he walked out.

What tears me apart most is that there was nothing at all that indicated that there was anything wrong so it was a terrible shock. It wasn't just us children who thought that; my mother and all my friends felt exactly the same. I've gone over and over the days leading up to it ever since and I still don't understand how he could plan something like that without giving us any hint that things were so wrong. The night before he left we had a very warm and normal evening at home and I even remember him being affectionate towards my mother; I saw them kissing at one stage. What a cold-hearted actor to be able to carry on like that when he was about to leave us all!

He left 13 years ago and now, aged 25 I still haven't got over it or seen him again. I've recently been prescribed antidepressants; that's how much it messed me up. I'm still so angry with him.

## Mental breakdown

With a mental breakdown the person will leave because they need to escape themselves and their lives. It's possible for someone experiencing a mental breakdown to hide it really well from friends and even family so do give it consideration before you dismiss it.

People often think that someone who's suffering from depression is simply feeling sad and needs to pull themselves together. The media will often report it like that, particularly when celebrities are diagnosed with it and their pampered lives are compared to the starving children of Africa. However depression, caused by a chemical imbalance in the brain, is a form of mental illness, not an extreme form of sadness. Someone suffering from it can no more pull themselves together than a person who's broken both legs can walk. However in time, and with the right care, it's an illness that people can make a good recovery from.

A person who's suffering from mental illness needs care, as with any other form of illness. If things have got really bad it may be necessary to have them committed to a hospital for their own safety or the safety of others. However in most cases short-term medication, counselling and rest can get the patient back to normal within weeks. Give them this space and keep the door open for when they're ready to return. Try not to resent them for the extra pressure on you; they can't help it. Children can be told that brains can get sick like every other part of the body and that, like with other illnesses, sick brains do get better.

## Charlotte's story:

I'd always been pretty dismissive of people with depression; I thought it was self-indulgence, although now I understand it I think I'd had it to some degree all my life. I'm a 'bubbly' person with a real passion for life, or that's how people think of me, but I've always had pretty extreme mood swings. About four years ago the bad times started to last longer and were much worse and it became more difficult to put on the charade of being happy. I was feeling really low most of the time and I found it a challenge just to stay awake. I went to the doctor, really because of the tiredness, but she asked me some more questions and I burst into tears in front of her. She diagnosed depression and suggested medication and time off work. But that seemed too dramatic so I thought I'd simply try harder not to be so miserable. But it got worse and worse.

One day I found myself sitting on the sofa not really sure whether I'd been asleep or where the time had gone. After that I had to be signed off work, as I didn't seem able to absorb any information. I'd try and watch TV but I couldn't understand what was happening, the same with reading, I couldn't even understand short newspaper articles. I was very suicidal at one stage but was still well enough to understand that it would be very wrong for the children, but eventually I felt so low and such a waste of space that I came to the conclusion that they would be much better off without me. I just needed to escape some-how. I drove for miles one night, not really sure where I was going. I had visions of sitting on a sunny beach and tried to find one; it was Halloween and past midnight!

During most of this time my friends and my work colleagues saw me as this lively happy person. One even described me as having amazing energy. Perhaps part of the reason I was so tired was the effort of hiding it. They were nearly all really shocked when I was signed off sick and one never spoke to me again, he was so convinced I was slacking off work. Many people still say to me that they think depressives should keep busy and working as a way of helping themselves but if you're really ill with it, working is not an option. It really bugs me when people criticise celebrities who have depression, as it shows the prejudice and ignorance that still surrounds it. It's not about how good your life is, that's irrelevant to the illness, it's about your brain going wrong and plunging you into a hole.

## Practical arrangements for a crisis situation

If you find yourself suddenly the lone parent in a home that you previously shared with your spouse you will need to estab-lish your legal position immediately. It will be very tempting to bury your head in the sand and hope the problems will go away; but if you do that you'll make your situation far worse.

Take a good look at your income and your outgoings; some may no longer be necessary. You may also find that your tax bill is reduced if there's only one adult in the house-hold and you may be entitled to benefits (particularly if your spouse is ill).

If your spouse has walked out he or she still has a responsibility to pay for the children's upkeep. In many countries this can be enforced legally, but only resort to this if your ex won't cooperate through any other means. Also look at other ways of increasing your income to help you balance your budget. If you can you need to avoid moving at such an emotional time but it's a better option than running up debt (which will then affect your ability to get credit) or getting evicted and being made homeless.

If you're in rented accommodation you need to ensure that you can pay the rent and that the property is put into your name. If you own your home check whose name is on the deeds. If you can't meet the mortgage payments speak to your lender immediately. Most are sympathetic if people let them know the situation before they run up debt and they may be able to suggest some ways to help (eg, interest-only repayments until you can afford it, extending the term to bring the payments down). If, realistically, you're not going to be able to afford your home by yourself they may even put off some of the payments until you've sold the property and found a cheaper one. This way you'll have your lender on your side and you'll be able to buy again. Tell them what you need to get through this. The worst they can say is no but it's in their interest to help you avoid running up debt so they're normally very helpful in coming to an arrangement that will suit you.

Try not to discuss these practical and financial problems in front of your children. They're not able to help and you'll just increase their stress.

# CHAPTER 4

## THE LEGAL PROCESS AND SPLITTING YOUR ASSETS

- Why do it differently?
- How to use lawyers
- The law and children
- DIY divorce
- Dividing up your money
- Dividing up your possessions
- Preparing for new partners
- The pitfalls that will make it bitter

Have a good look at your coffee table. How much is it worth to you? How about £20,000 ($40,000) plus a year's bitter argument and children so distraught that they'll never get over it? That's what you risk if your divorce gets acrimonious and you start to fight over your assets.

# Why do it differently?

When warring couples can't come to a financial agreement between them the court is asked to decide. The court will aim to minimise the drop in living standards for the children and provide a family home for the parent who is considered the primary carer. That sounds child friendly, doesn't it? It isn't, unless you're very wealthy or one of you already has a new partner to share their future living expenses.

The above arrangement often leaves fathers with very little, and certainly not enough to provide a home that could be shared with his children. This creates the need for those horrible Sunday afternoon access visits mentioned in the previous chapter. The children don't enjoy it, the mother makes it as difficult as she can and the father eventually gives up as no one is getting anything out of it.

I've already explained why you should stop thinking in terms of having a 'right' to your children, but instead recognise that your children have a right to *both* their parents. This principle is also relevant here, as it means that the financial arrangement should prioritise the need for both parents to have a home that the children can live in. That's much more important to your children's happiness than their living standards. If you leave your spouse with only enough money to eek out a miserable existence in a grotty bedsit or tiny apartment, while you keep the family home, you make it impossible for him (usually him) to be the dad your children need him to be. The children will not be able to hang out with him in the natural comfortable way that they should and eventually the stress of the situation will lead all but the most determined to give up.

## Greg's story:

I loved my kids; I was so proud and happy when they were born. Things started to go wrong soon after. My wife became just a mum and there didn't seem any love left for me. One day, when they were about six and eight, we had this huge fight and I left. I tried to be a good dad and gave them the family home and enough to live on. But it became a real struggle for me. I was doing so much over-time, just to be able to afford to live, that sometimes I wouldn't have a day off for weeks which meant I couldn't see the kids. My ex told them that I just couldn't be bothered to see them. It makes my stomach churn to think how that must have made them feel; it was a wicked thing to do to me and an evil thing to do to them.

The few times I did have them I never knew what to do with them. I couldn't take them back to my place; it was a pit and there was nothing to do there. Instead we wandered round the shops, but I couldn't afford to buy them anything, or we went to the park, even though it was freezing cold. I think everyone started to dread the visits and my ex made things as difficult as she could. Eventually I gave up; it just wasn't worth the upset it was causing me or the kids.

To represent your children's best interests you need to take full responsibility for ensuring that both of you are able to provide a home. It probably won't be as good as the one you have now and there will be some disruption, but in the long run children do not rate houses and localities over the chance to spend time with the people they love and need most in the world, and that includes their friends.

# How to use lawyers

I never used a lawyer in my divorce and several years on I know it was the best decision I ever made. That's probably the antithesis of the advice you'll be given elsewhere so I'll explain why.

Amicable divorces can be made acrimonious by just one visit to a bad lawyer. I'm sure there are some great ones out there who help people through divorce. My experience, and that of almost everyone I spoke to, is the opposite. And even the good ones will charge you, a lot. Remember your family has a fixed pot of money that now needs stretching between two homes. Anything you spend on lawyers to fight over it will reduce that amount. People who insist on fighting on no matter what (and many do) will keep running up bills until they run out of money. The McCartney divorce is rumoured to have cost him £30 million ($60 million) in his settlement to Heather but more than £60 million ($120 million) in legal costs and loss of earnings (this sort of fight takes more than money from you).

How can you ensure that you get what's 'legally yours' without a lawyer? You don't. Instead you recognise that the settlement in which you 'win' is the one which provides a happy secure future for your children. That means setting aside the idea of grabbing as much money as you can and punishing your ex. My way you might get less than a court would give you, particularly if you're female, but the pot of money available to provide a happy life for your children will be significantly larger. My ex and I were not wealthy; but the reason we were able to provide two homes, when most of our richer friends and relatives struggled, was because we didn't waste £100,000 ($200,000) on lawyers' fees fighting over what little we had.

Aside from the cost, I've heard many stories of lawyers making things worse by trying to maximise their income instead of helping you to come to a quick agreement. Lawyers are paid by the hour so effectively, the moment you engage them, you put them on an incentive scheme to make your divorce as acrimonious as possible. The worse it becomes the more they can charge you for sorting it out.

### John's story:

When my wife and I got divorced every little thing was argued out between the lawyers in hundreds of letters; it was a complete waste of time and money. My ex-wife got legal aid and I didn't so she wasn't bothered. I think I spent around £10,000 ($20,000) in legal fees and the only reason it wasn't much more was because I gave up fighting, as I could see it going on for years and it was obviously cheaper to just to give in.

One trick that a bad lawyer will use, that I experienced myself, is to suggest that you can get a divorce earlier than two years by citing unreasonable behaviour. I was told by a lawyer that things I found mildly irritating could, if presented 'properly', result in a successful unreasonable behaviour case. I was in no rush to get divorced yet the two lawyers I saw both suggested it and, although my husband had his share of bad habits, I don't honestly think they were any worse than mine. We were simply not compatible any more, but a divorce on that basis doesn't involve a lot of fighting, so the lawyers fixed on what they thought would be a way to increase what they were paid. I walked out in disgust which, from the look on their faces, was not a common reaction.

Good lawyers will suggest that you resolve all the issues between you by attending mediation. Yet studies have shown that only a third of their clients were told that this was the cheapest and quickest way to resolve disputes. Mediation will cost you less than half what a lawyer will cost you. There is now talk in some countries of making it compulsory for all but cases of domestic violence.

## Mike's story:

I thought the divorce was going fine. We settled on a fair split of the money and our stuff and we even had a lovely evening together where we discussed what went wrong, without any bitterness, and agreed to stay friends. I told her I'd always be there for her if she needed me. Then my wife went to see a lawyer 'just to be on the safe side'. He persuaded her that she could get much more and I'm afraid I told her to get lost, as it was totally unreasonable and would have left me with virtually nothing. After that it was all out war. I broke my collarbone and that was the week she insisted I retrieve my stuff from the loft where she'd stored it. I went up there and fell through a hole in the floor that she'd covered up with my jacket. I was in agony and some of my friends thought I should tell the police. I was horrified and became clinically depressed.

Although I didn't do it I now think it's worth drawing up your own separation agreement, particularly if the financial settlement between you is not final (eg, if you agree to a transfer of cash between you at a later date). You should get the agreement witnessed by a lawyer. This is because, once divorced, you will not be able to go back and enforce the agreement unless it's already in writing. To avoid the pitfalls I've mentioned, go and see your lawyers (you may want one each) together with your separation agreement and refuse to get into discussions about the divorce itself, the grounds for the divorce or how he or she could improve things for one of you. If that lawyer insists find another; preferably one that immediately checks that you've either been through mediation or come to an agreement between yourselves. Emphasise that you do not want the lawyer to advise you of your rights or to represent either of you in the divorce. What you're instructing them to do is simply to get the agreement between you formalised and witnessed so that you're protected if your spouse decides to forget about it.

## Wendy's story:

Our lawyers hated us. Neither of us needed to get divorced straight away; we were happy to wait two years to be eligible for that to be the reason, but we did want things finalised between us. Although our marriage was over we saw no reason to involve other people in how we managed the separation; we wanted to keep control of our lives. We therefore wrote our own separation agreement which included things such as lists of how our possessions would be divided. We then went to a lawyer to get it made legal. Because we'd already agreed everything between us the legal bill was only £250 ($500) and we then paid court costs of £50 ($100) (in Scotland in 2003) when the divorce went through two years later. Of course there were other costs, such as buying and selling property, but the divorce itself cost us only £300 ($600).

Many women assume that they will do really well financially by going to court, but nothing is certain. By contesting what you're offered, your husband will be compelled to go to lawyers too and they may advise him, as is often the case, that he's being too generous and if the court agrees your actions could result in you getting considerably less than you turned down, and you'll have to pay thousands of pounds in legal fees for the pleasure. If you do decide to go to court first check with an independent mediator, not your lawyer or your friends, that you have grounds for your belief that the settlement is unfair and make every effort to resolve the dispute out of court.

## The law and children

Do try to decide the practical arrangements for your children yourselves (as described in the last chapter) and only resort to asking the court to decide for you as a last resort.

Courts will normally give the primary carer role to the mother, even when the father had been the primary carer. The younger the children are the more likely this is to be the case. The only exceptions are where there is evidence of real problems such as mental health issues, drug addiction or physical abuse. Care may also be given to the father if the mother has walked out and not been in contact for a length of time. This is because the courts try to cause as little disruption to children as possible so they don't want to change the care arrangements once the children are settled.

The reasons behind the breakdown of the marriage are usually not taken into account in deciding where the children live. This is one time the law and I agree: the sort of spouse you are is irrelevant to whether you should be given care of your children.

In most cases the assignation of primary carer role does not make that parent a 'single' parent. The other parent usually retains a legally right to a say in the way their children are brought up and related issues such as their education.

The court can decide that neither of you are suitable parents if the serious accusations you make about each other are proved. However few courts will want to take children away from their parents unless they consider them to be in danger.

If your ex is not giving you access to your children in the first instance you should sit down and talk to them to find out why. What excuses are they using? If possible get them to attend counselling so a professional outsider can spell out to them the harm that they're doing to their children by denying them their right to both their parents. If this fails you will need to attend court to enforce your rights but even then your ex can still make things very difficult and poison your children's minds so that they don't want to maintain a relationship with you. However in the longer term children grow up to see things more fairly and take a very harsh view of the parent who has made it impossible for them to share their childhood with their other parent.

A court will not necessarily rule that children have to spend time with both their parents. Sometimes they'll suggest a 'time out' from one parent for a period of time with regular reviews put in place. This is because if the child doesn't want to see Mum or Dad a judge may decide it is in the interest of the child to be free of the worry for a good length of time.

The courts will usually resolve disputed child support payments and visiting rights and both parties can go back to court if these court orders are breached. However it is not legally acceptable for the parents to use either as a way of enforcing the other (eg, a mother cannot stop visiting rights because the father hasn't paid support and a father cannot stop paying support because the mother has stopped access visits).

Child support awarded by the courts can also vary a lot. I've heard of two examples where the court awarded only a nominal amount in maintenance (5p, 10¢, a year per child in one case and 1p, 2¢, a year per child in the other). These nominal awards are made where the courts recognise the parent's continued responsibility to pay for their children but don't feel a financial settlement is currently justified. Although the money is therefore of no use at all the recognition is important, as it gives you the right to go back to court and get the amount increased if you can prove the circumstances have changed.

## Grandparents

In most countries grandparents have no legal rights over their grandchildren. It's therefore up to the parents how much contact they have after a divorce. If your ex is still sharing responsibility for your children you can assume he or she will include his or her parents. However if your ex has no contact with your children, for whatever reason, the relationship your children have with your ex-in-laws will be down to you. Like with parents, your overriding consideration should be the happiness of your children. If their father has abandoned them it is cruel to take their grandparents away from them too, even if you don't get on with them. The only circumstances you might want to avoid this contact is if it might put your safety (and that of your children) at risk in cases of physical abuse.

## What's in a name?

After all the arrangements have been finalised women are commonly still left with one hangover from the marriage which creates a dilemma: their married name, which can feel like a label that states that they belong to their ex. Apart from the professional and practical problems it creates, if a mother changes her surname back to her maiden name then she'll have a different surname from her children which can be awkward for everyone. I know many mothers who've been assumed to be unrelated to their own children because they didn't share a surname. Consequently many women want to get rid of their married name but don't want their children to have a different name from them. In stepfamilies the many different surnames that can exist within it are often the most concrete reminder that this not a 'natural' family and many mothers, given the option, would happily change everyone's name to that of the stepfather so they could all pretend to be one family.

Changing the children's surname can create it own problems. Children over a certain age, and this can be quite young, will feel attached to their name: it is part of their identity. As boys, particularly, get older they will see their name as part of their heritage. Children do not usually want to wipe their father out of their lives in the way their mother might, even if the mother had the 'right' to do it. It is therefore nearly always better for children to be left with the name they were born with. The exceptions are where you need to disappear because of violent behaviour and where the father has ignored his children from a young age (at his instigation). Where a new partner is willing to take on previously fatherless children and give his name to them I can see many advantages to changing the children's surname and very few drawbacks. The children are likely to benefit from the feeling that they're part of a real family and accepted in the same way as natural children. However I would always check if the children were happy to change their name before you did it.

## DIY divorce

I'd always assumed that DIY divorce would be a bit like doing the conveyancing on your property yourself; possible but difficult and time consuming and not to be recommended. Laws vary but in many countries it's now as simple as applying for a passport (without the need for a dodgy photo). The standard procedure is to go to your local court (the address will be on the internet and in the phone book) and request a form. This will come with clear notes for guidance and the court officials (civil servants, nothing scary) should be happy to help.

You record the details of your marriage and give the grounds for the divorce. You will not usually need to complete the details about your finances if you've come to an amicable agreement between the two of you. Similarly with childcare arrangements; the court will only get involved if you can't agree. When you've completed the form you pay the court fee and they send a copy to your spouse. If the court is content that you have grounds you're granted a decree. There is usually no need for you to attend court. The divorce will then be made final around six weeks later. Do make sure you get a copy of that final document, as there have been cases where people have been found guilty of bigamy because they failed to go through this final stage.

An amicable divorce, where you agree everything without asking the court to decide for you, will take just a few months (expect around six) and cost you about the same as a good meal for two in an expensive restaurant. I suggest you go and have one. However much you want it, when the court document arrives telling you you're divorced, you'll probably feel very low. Everyone is different but I felt like I'd received an official certificate of failure. If you do feel overjoyed try to remember that to your children it's likely to represent sadness and seeing you celebrate may feel like you don't care about the upset you've caused. Greg told me, 'When my parents' divorce came through my mother held a party and displayed a framed copy of the decree absolute in our hallway. To my sister and me it would have been no less painful than if she'd partied on the death of a much-loved relative and framed the death certificate. We had to walk past it every day for the rest of our childhood.'

## Choose your grounds carefully

You'll need to prove that your marriage has broken down irretrievably for reasons that, in most countries, include adultery, unreasonable behaviour (or something similar) and a category that involves no blame being assigned. This is usually a set number of years living apart, commonly two. Your court will be able to advise you.

If you want to make this as painless as possible I strongly recommend that you go for grounds that don't introduce blame. On the form you state, 'The parties to the marriage have lived apart for a continuous period of at least two years [check what is needed] immediately preceding the presentation of the petition and the respondent consents to a decree being granted.' In the particulars you simply state 'On [insert date], the petitioner left the matrimonial home after it was agreed we could no longer live together as husband and wife. We have not lived together since that date.'

I know that you'll want to cite adultery if your spouse has cheated on you, but you're reading this book because you want to make things as easy as possible for your children, and that means working really hard to avoid antagonising your spouse. And strangely enough, many people don't like to be named as an adulterer, even if they are one, and may cross petition by citing unreasonable behaviour to prove that you're actually worse than them (see the next paragraph). So check with your spouse to see if it's going to cause additional upset. I can understand how irritating that sounds but this is not about expressing your anger, or getting public recognition for your spouse's crime at your children's expense.

What happens when you tell someone that they're useless/lazy/selfish (insert your spouse's failings)? Do you really expect your spouse to respond to an unreasonable behaviour petition with something on the lines of 'Fair point: I am a worthless human being. You can have your divorce. I don't deserve to be married to such a wonderful person as you'? I'm guessing that your spouse will have a little more life in them than that and will angrily try to defend themselves by arguing that your behaviour was worse than theirs. Assuming you're not a frustrated Big Brother contestant, having people pass judgement over your most intimate behaviour will not be a lot of fun. In fact you'll probably find it the worst experience of your life. If by some strange quirk of nature you married someone who would rather forget your bad habits (why are you divorcing them?!) their lawyer will consider it their job to wheedle it out of them.

You may believe that this can't apply to you: that you've done nothing that would justify an unreasonable behaviour petition. Think again. Even if you're a saint a 'good' lawyer, to 'protect' their client, will find something that they can spin to make you sound like the spouse from hell. That time you told your husband that his brother was quite dishy will be interpreted in legal documents as 'the Respondent has declared sexual interest in the Petitioner's near relatives.' And that new sex toy you tried to use once to spice things up, to the distaste of your wife, will become 'the Respondent has displayed deviant sexual behaviour.' Not forgetting that time you got up with a terrible hangover and didn't shower; 'the Respondent's drink problem has led to deterioration in their personal hygiene.'

Fun will be had but it will be by the lawyers as they fleece you for hundreds of pounds an hour while they enjoy the most devastating personal and intimate attacks by the two of you on each other. Your children will be terrified because as it gets nasty you will not be able to keep it from them and worst of all, if things get very serious, your children may be asked to give evidence. I'm sure you've seen how bad things can get from cases in the media. Perhaps you thought that sort of behaviour was confined to celebrity divorces? I'm afraid it is actually typical of divorce cases where one or both of the people involved are so angry that they're more interested in 'winning' than in being in any way fair or reasonable. They either have no understanding of the effect of their behaviour on their children or simply don't care. Anger is an emotion that can block out all rational thought and greed can make people forget their morals.

If the court accepts the evidence presented it will be a matter of official public record that you're incestuous, smelly, a pervert (or whatever crimes you're alleged to have committed). It's difficult to find a way to be the united supportive parents you need to be after you've endured that sort of battle. Is that really worth a quick divorce or the chance to get it publicly acknowledged that squeezing the toothpaste from the middle is wrong? (By the way, if that is the reason you want a divorce I suggest you get one with a pump.)

The only reason you should risk introducing blame to the divorce when you have children is if your divorce laws make it mandatory (some places still do) or if you want to remarry straight away. In those circumstances you should try, calmly, to agree that one of you or even both of you (to keep the peace) cite adultery. Don't tell your children that this is what you're doing and remember it is just a legal clause.

### Emma's story:

My parents divorced when I was eight after Mum found out Dad had been sleeping with her sister. Mum threw him out and my brother and I only saw him twice after that. Both times my mother quizzed us on everything we did and we felt we had to make out that we hated spending time with him, as it felt disloyal to her to tell her the truth; that it was lovely to see him and how much we missed him. So after the second visit she told him that we didn't want to see him any more and she refused him all contact. She proudly told everyone that she was protecting us from him.

I'm 24 now and I still have to stop myself crying if I smell the aftershave he wore. I want to contact him but feel it's been too long now and I don't know where to start. I know Dad was in the wrong but he was a great father. Looking back, there was no need for Mum to have stolen him from us. I think that was worse than Dad's crime. She married again but I only had one dad. I can't forgive her for that and Mum and I barely speak now.

# Dividing up your money

You should agree how you'll divide your money and your possessions before you start the legal process of the divorce. The best time to do it is when you physically split through a separation agreement. The court then doesn't need to be involved. I can't tell you exactly how to divide your money, as everyone's circumstances are different. All I can give you are the questions and principles that should influence what you decide.

Unless you're rich, both of you will have to make sacrifices and drop your standard of living, significantly. In addition, this is the 21st century, so the following also apply:

1. Both of you are responsible for your children's future happiness. An agreement that causes bitterness or leaves one of you much worse off than the other is bad for your children.
2. The agreement should treat both of you like the equal adults that you are and not favour one over the other based on gender.
3. Both of you should leave the marriage in the sprit of the agreement you made when you entered it. Unless it was clearly a financial arrangement, as opposed to an emotional one, you should continue to treat it that way, not try to make money out of it.

You should therefore start from the assumption that the fairest solution is to assess your joint wealth and divide it equally between the two of you. Your joint wealth is usually the amount of equity in your home plus savings, investments and the value of high-worth items (such as cars). From this figure you take away any debts and the cost of releasing the money. As you're both capable of earning money, and child-care continues to be a joint responsibility, the opening assumption is that there is no need for further payments from one of you to the other. There are many very valid reasons why you should shift from this starting point but it does give you the basis from which to work.

While I see absolutely no moral reason for a person to gain financially from being married (surely love should be the one thing we don't pay for) nor should anyone suffer financially from it. To identify how you reach a point where no one gains or loses and that creates the best solution for your children you should ask yourselves the following questions to determine how much you need to deviate from the opening assumption:

1. Where will the children live and what proportion of their time will be spent at each home (see previous chapter)? If one of you (whichever it is) will take on a larger portion of care, payments will need to be agreed (taking account of any state benefits linked to the children). The primary carer may also be given proportionately more of the joint wealth. If the children are only staying with their dad one week in four, for example, then in that home they may share a bedroom but have their own rooms at

their mum's. The extra money needed to provide that accommodation may be returned to the father when the children leave home.

2. Do you both work? Are you both capable of working? Is there a large disparity in your incomes? Has this been affected by one of you staying at home part or full time to take care of children? Staying at home either part- or full-time to care for children during the critical career age of the 20s and 30s will impact on long-term income and this needs to be recognised in the settlement between you. A lower income will affect how much mortgage or rent that parent can take on. It may mean that one of you takes proportionately more of the joint wealth to compensate.

3. Do you pay for childcare or have one of you been their only source of care? Do you wish/need to pay for childcare in the future to enable you both to work full-time? If you're agreed that one of you should stay at home to look after the children then the other will need to pay them maintenance and compensate them for the effect on their career.

4. Do you both have adequate pension arrangements or has one of you been relying on the other? If one of you was reliant you should immediately start to organise your own pension but you are entitled to half the pension earned during the marriage. See below.

5. How much does it cost to 'run' your children? Are all these costs still necessary and affordable? Remember, when your children look back on their childhood they will rate a happy and secure home

life (with both their parents) far higher than ballet lessons or even private education but you do need to recognise that friends and these activities are important and try to minimise their disruption during this time.

6. Is there enough money to provide you both with an adequate home? If not you need to work hard to find a way round it. First check you're not setting up false barriers, such as demanding living standards that are not achievable. Consider ways of earning more money, such as taking in lodgers and selling some of your possessions, to meet costs. It may be tempting to go ahead with a divorce in these circumstances, on the basis that the new arrangements are only temporary. However this hardship will come at the most critical time in the divorce, when your children are adjusting to it, and it will set the new routine. It's therefore preferable to delay things as long as possible to give yourselves time to solve the financial problem.

7. Has one of you got a new partner to share the cost of the new home? If this is the case, and the other partner would struggle to afford a decent new home on their own then, for the sake of the children, the split should give the 'single' spouse a larger share of the money to help them set up a new home.

There are two other major exceptions to the above:

- If one of the parents has an addiction that haemorrhages large amounts of money then, until the problem is resolved, any money assigned to the addict will be wasted rather than go to providing a good home for the children. This should be reviewed immediately once there is evidence that the problem is resolved.

- When one or both parents are very wealthy, an equal split is not necessary for the sake of the children. After ensuring that the children are able to enjoy a standard of living not unreasonably disparate from one parent to the other, the parents should then simply leave the marriage with what they brought or contributed to it.

Try to avoid one of you being left owing the other one money. However sincere you are about repayment it can create a point of antagonism between you and in my experience is rarely (if ever) repaid.

## Pensions

In many countries pensions are seen as a joint financial asset and courts give the divorcing couple the right to half the pension earned during the marriage. This makes sense morally where the other person was relying on that pension for their own retirement and sacrificing their career to care for the children or the home. Pensions should therefore be included in your division of joint assets.

If you both have similar pension entitlements I think it is easiest if you both leave the marriage with the pension you have without establishing a claim over the other pension. If your pension arrangements are not equal enough for this to be fair you have three options:

1. Agree a proportion of the pension to be assigned to the other based on the length of the marriage and the contributions made to the pension (including those of the employer) during the life of the marriage.
2. Cash the pension in (may not be possible) and each takes half to invest in a new pension.
3. Get the pension valued and include that in the financial settlement between you (again based on the length of the marriage and the contributions made to the pension during the life of the marriage). This will allow the person with the pension to benefit from the continuation of it and allow the other to buy their own pension.

The third option, if you can afford to do it, is usually the most sensible financially. It is normally a bad idea to cash pensions in, as most have large set-up costs built into them and the first option means that your ex-spouse continues to be linked to you financially. This link can cause future problems between you, as many people resent the idea of their ex having a continued right to part of their pension, even if they fully accept the moral justification for it. Whatever option you think suits you both best, see your financial advisor to check on the implications and make sure it's written clearly into your separation agreement.

## Dividing up your possessions

Dividing up possessions can get very emotional, particularly if you've been together any length of time. Objects can be very powerful reminders of happier times, hopes and dreams.

Whatever method you adopt don't do it (or even discuss it) in front of the children and come back to it later if one or both of you starts to get upset.

How you divide up the children's things is dependent on their age. If they're young you should agree to split toys, etc, so that they have familiar, much-loved things in both homes. Older children should be given the choice of where they want their possessions while trying to limit the amount of packing they need to do by getting duplicates where possible.

One of my mistakes was not being more prescriptive on this point at the start. The result was that my daughters insisted on packing up pretty much all their stuff each time they moved, rather than accepting that their two homes would be different. They owned two nearly identical pairs of jeans, but they still wouldn't leave a pair in each house. We ensured that they had things like hair dryers, TVs and even 'essentials' like hair straighteners in each home, yet today, six years on, Ella has just come home with five large bags of stuff which will take her days to unpack. I really thought she would learn to travel light. I was mistaken; if anything she's got worse.

As furniture is expensive, and children tend not be too bothered whether they keep it or have new stuff, it should be included in the same agreement as the rest.

Where items have a high second-hand value, such as expensive jewellery and original works of art, your decision to sell or keep will depend on how stretched your finances are going to be and how attached you are to the items.

You should also look at the value of any vehicles you have (cars, boats, caravans, etc) and ensure an equal division between you. This should be fairly straightforward as with houses; it's easy to get the financial worth of these items if resold. This split should not be dependent on whether you both drive, simply on value.

If you hide your possessions or money in order to keep more than your share then remember that you're cheating your children and are setting things up to be very bitter. At some stage your children will almost certainly discover what you've done and you'll be judged by them and are very unlikely to be forgiven.

Where possessions are genuinely related to work they should stay with the person whose work they relate to and should not be included in the separation agreement. This is likely to include things such as laptop computers, vans and tools, reference books and even office furniture. It's probably worth listing them so that there are no misunderstandings.

It's not uncommon for people to adopt the attitude, 'I don't care. Take the bloody lot!' What they actually mean is that they're currently in too much pain to give it any attention. Respect that and leave it a while if you can. When emotions have settled, and they're faced with the reality of how much it costs to set up a home from scratch, they'll feel differently. This initial reaction doesn't give you the right to take everything. Don't throw stuff out, particularly personal stuff, until everyone has calmed down. Instead try and store it if you have to and offer it back when things are less fraught.

If one of you is leaving to live with someone else they probably don't need as much stuff (or even have room for it) so it makes sense for them to take much less. The 'single' spouse will then have to buy much less and that will increase the pot of money available to provide homes for your children, so you both win.

If you've not been married long (less than five years) and one of you came to the relationship with a house full of furniture or other possessions, and the other pretty much nothing, then it is fairer for the former to retain that furniture.

Check with your spouse whether you can agree a simple solution for some or all of your stuff to be divided. My ex took the upstairs furniture and I took the downstairs. You might also be able to do some quick bartering: 'You can take the big plasma in the living room if I can take the two smaller ones.'

## The auction

Invariably, even with agreements like those above, you will still have a lot of things that need dividing up (think of them as hundreds of potential arguments). One way to manage the division is a variation on a Dutch auction. This method takes account of both the financial and emotional value each of you have for your things, and should give you a split that you're both reasonably happy with, but don't expect it to be a precise science.

1. Go through your home together and list everything you have by room, and make a special note of things that might be worth selling to release money.

2. As you go round agree on some groupings as you don't really want to list every item of cutlery or every figurine. You can also assume that all personal possessions remain yours (eg, clothes, toiletries, mobile phones and MP3 players, low-value jewellery, plus non-valuable collections). Books, CDs, games and videos should be dealt with individually on the assumption that the person who

bought or was given it should keep it. If you can't agree on any of them (memories do fade) then buy another. Similarly with photos and photo albums; it really is cheaper to make a copy of photos you both want than have a fight over them.

3. Once you've agreed the list make a copy so that each of you can go through it (in your own time) and decide on the following:

> X – I don't want it
> 1 – I'll have it if he or she doesn't want it
> 2 – I would like to keep it but not a top priority
> 3 – It means a lot to me. I really want it

NB: You're each allowed to give only a third of items a number 3 and a third of items a number 2, so you'll need to add up all the items and divide the total by three to agree on those maximums before you start.

Be honest. This is not about winning, it's about coming to an agreement that you both find fair and works for your new circumstances. Think about what you really want and be practical. I made the mistake of taking the dining table which just got in the way so I later gave it back.

4. Arrange to meet to go through the list when you're both ready, feeling reasonably calm and the children are elsewhere. First one of you reads out all the things that they've given a 3 mark to. It makes no difference which one of you it is. The other stops them each time that they have a 3 against the same item. You both then record with a tick that you need to discuss it

later and carry on. When you've finished the 3s do the same with 2s and finally the 1s. The person who gives the highest number to items should be allocated them (although they can be part of future trades). If there are things that neither of you want arrange to get rid of them (sell them if you can, give them away or throw them out if they're junk).

5. Now start to discuss where your 3s match and try to divide them up between you. If you can't quickly agree a trade then move on to something else until you're just left with the difficult items. You'll then be able to see clearly what you have to barter with. Think about what matters to your spouse – is it sentimental to them or was it theirs before you were married? You'll almost certainly find that this attitude is repaid. If not, don't worry about it; instead give yourself points for being a good person, far more valuable than any of your material objects.

| Living room: | Sell? | Category | Matches | Agreed His | Agreed Hers |
|---|---|---|---|---|---|
| TV | | 2 | | ✓ | |
| DVD | | 2 | ✓ | | ✓ |
| Sofas | | 3 | | | ✓ |
| Bookcase | | 2 | | ✓ | |
| Original painting | ✓ | | | | |
| 3 vases | | 1 | | | ✓ |
| Music centre | | x | | ✓ | |
| Coffee table | | 3 | ✓ | | ✓ |
| 2 side tables | | 2 | | ✓ | |
| Plants | | 1 | | ✓ | |

Example of 'auction' list showing one room

During the bartering part of the auction neither of you is allowed to make demands without first making an offer: eg, 'Looking at this list again the lamps you want go with the sofas so it makes more sense for you to have them if you'll let me have the vases instead?' This bartering may feel like that bit in Monopoly where you trade property to get a full set – good: that will help keep the emotion out of it.

To keep things sweet you may have to bite your tongue a lot, and never assume that your spouse wants something just to get at you. Most people will act fairly if they feel they're being treated fairly. If they don't remember they're just things; things that have the potential for hurting your children if you fight over them.

If the above doesn't work for you and you start to argue about how things are split see a mediator not a lawyer.

### Jan's story:

My ex-husband and I had a really bitter divorce. Most of the furniture was mine before we married. It was antique stuff that I loved. It wasn't worth that much, probably a few thousand in total. However when we divorced my ex fought me for every stick of it. Eventually we had to split most of it but I wasn't going to let him have the coffee table. I knew he hated it and I loved it. At the end of the divorce I looked over the bill from the lawyer. The months of wrangling over that one table cost me just under £20,000 ($40,000), simply because I refused to budge. Looking back, he probably provoked me deliberately and it would have been far better to tell him to have the bloody table! We had been fairly well off. The divorce cost us every bit of equity in our house as well as all our savings. Worst of all the prolonged arguing had a devastating effect on our daughters just at the time they were all taking important exams.

## Pets

A friend of mine told me, 'We divided up our possessions pretty easily but deciding who kept our two dogs very nearly caused our amicable divorce to turn nasty. I worked from home, and the dogs were used to me being there, but my ex would rather have given them to someone else than let me keep them.'

Pets can cause as many arguments as money and children. Unlike children, sharing pets is not really an option. You need to consider three things with pets:

- Are they attached to the children? If so they should go to the same parent who will have the children most.
- Do they have a natural owner? Did one of you own them before your relationship started? Who bought them and who's looked after them most?
- Who's able to care for them best after the divorce? If the pet is a dog is one of you going to be at home more than the other?

Like with everything else, be sensitive to each other. If you get the pets give your ex plenty of chances to see them; let him or her take them for walks and give them first refusal to care for them when you go on holiday.

## Preparing for new partners

If you do succeed in keeping things amicable right through to when you're both living in separate homes don't assume that it will stay like that. New partners coming on to the scene often seriously disrupt previously very cosy arrangements.

Many of us don't want our exes but are still uncomfortable with the idea of them being with anyone else, however daft that sounds, so jealousy can come from both sides and happen even years after the divorce. It's pretty common for the person not to realise that they'll feel jealous until they see their ex with a new partner and then to hide that feeling even from themselves. They then try and pretend that their upset and anger is caused by something else. Leading up to separation, we can get so angry with someone, or irritated by their bad habits, that we stop appreciating that they do have good qualities and we don't realise that someone else could find them endearing enough to want to start a relationship with them. It can be a genuine shock when they start dating and make you reassess what you gave up, particularly if the new partner impresses you in some way.

Many people, men particularly, continue to have an active role in caring for their ex long after the divorce. This can include everything from helping out with odd jobs right the way through to going on holiday with their ex. Where there is little or no bitterness it may seem to make perfect sense to continue to support each other and make the children's home and life more comfortable in this way. Men have said to me, 'I still care about her so why shouldn't I help out? When I start dating my new girlfriend will just have to respect that.'

Fast forward a couple of years and the new girlfriend does not respect that because they understand better than their new man that it means he and his ex haven't yet let go of each other. Unless you make room for your new partner they'll leave too and you'll quickly bow to that pressure to prove your love. Your poor ex meanwhile won't understand why you're suddenly being so cold. Because of your friendly helpful behaviour your ex may, until this point, even have harboured hopes of a reconciliation and your new relationship may feel adulterous to them. Whether they have these hopes or not, your sudden change in behaviour will come at a time when they'll be feeling most vulnerable. I've seen many ex-wife and new wife lock horns because of this scenario and it will make things extremely uncomfortable for your children. Having argued for so many pages about keeping things friendly I'm now suggesting that you limit how friendly things are because, in every example I found, it lead to false hopes and expectations for the future.

New partners often offer a fresh and critical interpretation on the divorce settlement. 'I can't believe you let her keep the house/she makes you have the children so much/expects you to drive them to football matches...' The two of you might have been happy with what was agreed but someone else telling you that you've been taken for a mug can make you re-question things and become much less cooperative. Divorcees, particularly those who've reached middle age, are far more likely to be pragmatic about the need for money than romantic, starry-eyed younger lovers. Most people will put the need to provide for their children ahead of their own romantic needs so it doesn't make them mercenary. If your new partner loves you but finds that you don't have enough to provide the home they and their children need it can be a real deterrent to the relationship proceeding or make them very resentful of the agreement you reached.

## Gemma's story:

When I got divorced things were so amicable our lawyer actually told us, 'If all couples agreed things like you have then we'd be out of business.' Things stayed like that until my ex-husband married again three years later. As we'd both agreed that I should stay at home to care for our four children I was still reliant on him financially. We'd therefore decided that I should stay in the house until the children were adults (they were already teenagers) at which time we'd sell the house and divide the proceeds, but this wasn't put in writing; I trusted him. When Susan (his new wife) came on the scene she clearly resented the fact that I still lived in a large house and got my ex to tell me to sell it straight away or he'd stop paying the mortgage. That was just the start of the problems. I can't even speak to him now. The last time I tried, about a matter that affected our daughter, Susan answered and screamed down the phone at me.

Some people, often through guilt, are overly generous in the divorce settlement, only for their 'wronged' spouse to quickly get a new partner who then benefits disproportion-ately. If you're giving your spouse everything because of guilt try to think how you'd feel if they got married again within the next couple of years. You shouldn't assume that your spouse will spend the rest of their lives brooding over you, even if that's what they say or imply now; it's actually very arrogant to think that you're the only one they could ever love. And remember you can't ask for the money and furniture back if he or she quickly find happiness again. If they like being married then they'll probably find a new partner much quicker than you'd expect, most people do within five years however upset they were about the break-up. I've come across numerous guilt-ridden spouses who spent years struggling to stay in a marriage for their partner's sake, have then been very generous in the divorce settlement as a way of compensating their partner, only for the partner to be the one who finds love again very quickly. This has huge potential to open up bitterness between the couple as one struggles with nothing while the other lives in style with both the proceeds of the marriage and the wealth of being part of a couple again.

It's worth learning from the experiences of others who've made the mistake of leaving furniture and other possessions in their ex's house. Once you leave it's not your home any more and, by default, your ex will probably assume that those possessions are now his or hers. When you get a new home and go to claim back 'your' lawnmower you may find he or she won't let you have it; when you go to see your children you may find a new man or woman with their feet up on your chair, drinking wine out of your glasses and watching your TV. Unless you're sure this won't bother you make it clear who owns what now in your separation agreement, however cold-blooded you think that sounds.

## Andy's story:

I was unhappy for years but stayed with my wife until the children were teenagers, at which point I left. According to the children she cried pretty much non-stop for six months and she told me she'd never get over me. I felt so guilty that in the separation agreement I gave her all our money, the house, the furniture, everything.

Within two years she'd married again and is much happier than she ever was with me. We weren't suited but I now realise that it was no reason for me to take on all the blame. All that did was make us both unhappy; by doing the 'worst' and leaving her, I actually gave her the chance to find real love, which by staying with her I'd prevented. The children grew up in a house without any warmth, which I now think was plain daft. Sometimes you have to be cruel to be kind. No one should feel guilty because they've stopped loving someone, it happens and staying with them is doing no one any favours, least of all the children and partner you're trying to protect.

It's only now that she's married again that I can begin to think about finding someone for me and I'm really starting to resent the fact that my ex and her new husband have all my money. He's done nothing with his life and I've worked really hard so it's difficult not to feel the unfairness of it.

# The pitfalls that will make it bitter

The divorce and separation process is therefore pretty straightforward. Divide everything fairly and who can complain?

What is it that makes it so emotionally draining for everyone? What are the flash points for the bitterness that is nearly always a feature of divorce?

People commonly make the same mistakes. However amicable your divorce is now, unless you work very hard at it, you'll start to do one or more of the following three things and it will lead to disaster:

1. You'll create a cycle of bad behaviour. If you're petty and uncompromising because you're angry, or simply want to win all that you can, your spouse will behave the same way. Remember we reap what we sow; only sometimes we reap a whole crop that we weren't expecting.

   It usually starts as a small thing: 'He only wants that table because he knows I like it,' but it quickly spirals out of control unless one of you breaks the cycle. To avoid it, bite your tongue when irritated and give in on things that matter to him or her. If you do get angry, and you will, then apologise, even if the fault is not all yours. You'll find that compromise is usually repaid however bad things have got. If you're not biting your tongue so much and so often that it's nearly coming off then you're not doing it enough.

2. You'll start to demonise your spouse. Psychologists will tell you that there are two reasons why we do this: firstly to fall out of love with anyone, even someone who's died, you normally have to go through a stage when you're angry with them. This seems to help blast the love away by making us

focus on what we hated about them. Secondly most of us still think of divorce as a failure and there will be a lot of blame flying around, including from family and your children. It's very difficult to accept blame; our natural instinct is to deflect it on to someone else.

By demonising our spouse we're putting all the blame on to them for the failed marriage so that we can play the victim. Playing the victim is appealing because it deflects other people's anger away from us and elicits sympathy instead. It also allows us to feel helpless and not responsible for the hurt being caused, thereby making our own consciences feel better. This is such common practice that your friends will expect you to do it and may even start it off without your suggestion. Some of mine were shocked when they started the 'He's such a bastard' line and I responded, 'No. He irritates the hell out of me but that doesn't make him a bad man.' Like lawyers, friends can, unintentionally, makes things worse.

Your spouse may not be blameless but he or she's probably not a demon (unless your name's Buffy or you're a charmed one!). They're a person with a load of faults that you now find irritating because you've fallen out with each other. By demonising them you give yourself permission to treat your divorce as a battle that you need to win and you stop thinking of your spouse as a person who is probably going through a lot of pain. You also stop feeling responsible for minimising the bitterness in the divorce.

Instead of demonising your spouse, deal with them like you would a particularly irritating boss at work. Find someone (one or two friends not more) to bitch and download to but keep calm the rest of the time if you can and find ways round the conflict that make it possible for you all to get through it. If your spouse does lean more to the side of demon than most find a way of dealing with your anger that doesn't include your children. If you believe in a god then leave him or her to punish any wrong-doing, if you don't, then trust in karma; people who treat others badly are rarely happy in the long term.

3. One of you will decide you can't agree the divorce between you and go and see a lawyer. I've already told you of the dangers of lawyers. If things get really bad make an appointment to see a relationship counsellor or a mediator instead and agree to abide by his or her advice. Relationship counsellors are trained to help couples who are separating, as well as to help couples repair their relationships. If there's a waiting list find one privately; it will still cost you less than half what it would cost you to see a lawyer.

4. One of you finds a new boyfriend/girlfriend. New partners have the potential to cause a number of problems (jealousy and criticising the settlement are just two, see above) which is why I suggest, in all your arrangements, that you assume that both of you will form a new relationship at some stage and agree a separation agreement that neither of you can change.

If, after all this effort to keep things amicable, you still feel you have some anger to release then go back to those kick-boxing classes I recommended earlier, far more rewarding and fun than fighting over furniture. And if you really miss it, go and buy another coffee table that hasn't had your ex's dirty feet all over it. You'll be able to afford it because you won't have a massive legal bill to pay.

# Chapter 5

---

## The First Few Months

---

- Dealing with blame
- Setting the new rules
- Discipline
- Your new social life
- Sex as a single parent
- Coping with sole custody
- Becoming a time lord
- Making them feel loved

Whenever we meet someone new it's said that we make a judgement about them within seconds that will colour how we feel about them for ever. I think the same can be said of experiences. The first few months after separating will probably set the tone for your children's attitude to their new life. This is a period when emotions are high for everyone and with high emotion typically comes extreme behaviour. When angry with me my father used to tell me to 'Behave!' which assumed I knew what I was doing wrong. I'm pretty sure he was right most of the time. It's not so obvious what you're doing wrong when you, your ex and your children are struggling with the emotions that often follow separation like a massive tidal wave. It's only with the benefit of hindsight, and when the flood of emotions has passed, that most people can look back and see what they got right and wrong.

## Dealing with blame

Children, whatever age they are, will not understand why you divorced, even if everyone else, including next door's cat, saw it coming. They'll therefore try to understand it in the context of their own experiences.

Young children, in their more simplistic understanding of the world, tend to want to assign blame for things that go wrong. It's therefore very common for young children to take the blame on themselves for this disaster in their lives. This will happen even if you both stress that it's not true so often it sounds like your catchphrase. They might also deny that's what they believe. Blaming themselves for the divorce is a way for young children to protect themselves. The logic in a child's mind is that for things to go wrong someone must have been bad so therefore someone is to blame, if it's not the child's fault then the only other people to blame are one or both of the parents; if the parents are 'bad' then they stop being the child's protectors from the evils of the world and that makes life much more terrifying. A child might therefore feel more powerful and safer if they blame themselves. They will then look for ways to correct the mistakes they've made and so make sure the divorce doesn't happen, or if it does, work towards reconciliation, often for years.

As they get older, children are more likely to want to put the blame on to their parents. They will then think in terms of blaming one of you for all the wrongs that happen in their lives from then on. It's important that you both work to prevent that happening, however tempting it is if it's your ex being blamed (and rightly in the circumstances) rather than you. By doing that you're effectively taking away his or her parental authority, which will make it very difficult for your ex to be the parent the child needs.

You might also be feeling very guilty about what you've done, particularly during this period where the lives of the people you love are disrupted and when everything seems a terrible struggle. You may not have instigated the divorce but you may start going over your marriage to try to find something you could have done differently that would have prevented this horrible situation. It can be a very depressing time. Try not to feel too guilty; with less than 50 per cent of children born in wedlock and around 50 per cent of marriages ending in divorce, the chances of your children having married parents for ever are slim.

Many people defend themselves by going on the attack. With this type of person the guilt they feel over their behaviour will quickly go from apologetic to trying to find ways to try to make the partner (and even the children) they let down take on some of their guilt.

### Genny's story:

Clive and I were heading for divorce for years but we kept putting it off because of our two children. Clive was a bit of a snob and a bully and made it clear that he thought he was much better than me. It came to a head when we were attending a dinner party and, prior to leaving the house, Clive started to lecture me about my manners and whether the chocolates I was bringing were too downmarket for our hosts. I sat through that dinner party seething while he acted the affable dinner-party guest. When we got home I asked him to leave as soon as possible. He was really weepy and apologetic about his behaviour that night but I'd really had enough.

I found out recently, through a mutual friend, that Clive tells people that he was the one that instigated the separation because of our son Tim's bad behaviour which he said I failed to control or take 'direction' from him. Tim suffered from attention deficit disorder and was pretty difficult to live with sometimes but that was never mentioned in the divorce. When I spoke to other friends about it many of them told me similar stories. I suppose none of us, even as adults, like being publicly dumped and find it even more difficult to accept we're to blame for what happened. However I thought Clive publicly putting the blame on to a 12-year-old boy was pretty low.

## Setting the new rules

The two most important things to do at this time is to ensure that you avoid, as far as possible, any more animosity brewing between you and set a structure that gives your children the parenting they need. Setting rules can help you achieve both. I've already suggested a couple of headline rules that you should agree the moment you decide to separate:

- You both remain responsible for your children. Neither should take it on themselves to make major decisions without the other being involved.
- Neither of you is allowed to criticise or mock the other (or their new partner) in front of your children: that includes minimising arguments between the two of you in their presence.

You should now think about these in more detail to define what they will actually mean in practice, as well as identifying any other issues that you need to agree on. I think there are three main headline aims and principles that rules fall into: a recognition that neither of you has more rights over the children than the other, actions you can take to minimise the children's distress at the divorce and the need to provide a sound support structure for your children. Some of these overlap a little. As you read this book and think things through, you may come up with other principles that you believe will help your children and your peculiar set of circumstances.

Once you've got these headings it's then easier to think about what they mean on a day-to-day basis. What actions and behaviours would go against your aims and principles? What behaviour would annoy you and cause you to fall out with your ex? If the behaviour would annoy you it would probably annoy your ex too and anticipating spark points before they ignite conflict in this way is a very effective way of blocking it. Think too about what you think would upset or confuse your children in the new arrangements. Put yourself in their minds as much as you can and sit them down and listen to what they have to say to understand their worries. With some of the rules it's quite a good idea to let your children know that you have them. Rules are comforting things to children and make them feel safer. I gave my children permission to tell me to shut up if ever I was rude about their father or stepmother in front of them and explained why.

If one of you doesn't agree with a rule or the thinking behind it then they're unlikely to keep the rule so discuss it but obviously don't argue about it. To help you start this process, I suggest the following:

## We share responsibility for our children which means:

- If our children become ill or have an accident (particularly if taken to hospital) we will inform the other as a matter of urgency.
- If our children get into any trouble or are in danger (eg, go missing, are expelled from school, commit a criminal offence, are drinking underage, are taking drugs taking or get involved with the police) we will notify the other as soon as possible.
- Both of us take responsibility for ensuring that the other receives school reports and notifications about parents' evenings, school and other perform-ances and events that the children are involved in.
- Drastic haircuts or other changes to appearance for any of our children will first be agreed with the other parent.
- Neither of us will take the children out of the country without it first being agreed with the other but neither of us will refuse permission without genuine reason. (Reasons for refusing permission

might include critical exam periods, important family celebrations, medical problems, emotional problems or a fear of abduction.)

- We will inform each other if there are issues in our children's lives that may affect their emotional well-being (eg, death of a pet, remarriage, illness of the parent).
- We will take responsibility for ensuring that our children attend optician's, dentist's and doctor's appointments.

## We want our children to suffer as little as possible emotionally from the divorce so will strive to minimise any future conflict between us which means:

- The purpose of the relationship between us is now solely to give supportive care for our children. No issues from the marriage will be carried over into that new relationship. Those arguments are over and die with the marriage.
- We will accept with civility and consideration any new step-relations that our children now have.
- We will inform new partners of the rules between us and will actively help them to respect them.

## We want to give our children a sound support structure which means:

- If a child criticises the other parent (or partner) to us we will not agree or support the criticism but back up the absent parent and strive to repair the problem.

- If a child is behaving particularly badly the other parent will be informed and will back the other parent up. Where necessary we will both sit down together to address behavioural issues as a joint team.

- If one of us can't have the children when they are scheduled to we will not assume the other can. We remain responsible for finding care. However both of us will help each other out as much as possible in these circumstances.

It's sometimes difficult to judge what information you should share with your ex about the children, particularly if they're a harsher disciplinarian than you are. However a good yardstick to use is if you would be upset to have the information kept from you. Similarly if you have major news that might have an emotional impact on your children then you should alert your ex first so that they're prepared to offer any necessary support. One mother told me, 'My eight-year-old came back from his father's really upset one day. I asked him what the matter was and he told me that he wouldn't be seeing his dad the following weekend because he was getting married in the Caribbean.'

During the first few months incidents may happen that make you realise that you need more rules, or that the rules you set aren't working. Review and revise them as you think necessary. They're there to make this work, not to straitjacket you.

Sometimes you need to be flexible with the rules and with 'access' times. One of the things that causes children the most pain in a divorce is being torn away from their friends in order to see a parent because the parent demands that they get their 'time' without considering what the child needs. The more you demand your time with your children, irrespective of their social life, the more they'll resent you for it and grow away from you. One day soon they'll have a choice of whether to see you or not. If you find that your children are starting to resist coming to see you don't assume your ex is poisoning their minds as it's far more likely that you're taking them away from something in their life that they want to do, so sit down and find out what the real problem is. If you have your children at the weekend does it mean that they're missing out on parties, for example? Can you promise to ensure that you get them to these social events? You may think they're pretty unimportant but to a child, of whatever age, they're not and by dismissing their importance you're telling your child you're not interested in what they want, just in making sure you get your time with them. Of course it will be a hassle to chauffeur them around like this but remember your divorce caused the problem; your children just want to have the same childhood as the children of non-divorced parents.

### Mia's story:

My ex always phones our sons, every night, at 6 pm. The boys don't actually want to talk to him; they've got nothing to say and I have to really encourage them but sometimes we just leave the answerphone on now, as I've done what I can. I've told him not to call so often and so regularly but he just thinks I'm poisoning their minds. In fact I'm working really hard to stop the boys from resenting him. You can't demand affection; you have to show it but by forcing these conversations on the boys he's making himself into someone to dread rather than someone to love.

## Breaking the rules

Having set the rules, you'll both break them sometimes. When you do it apologise immediately to your ex or your children (as appropriate), eg, 'Sorry, I didn't mean to say that about Dad; I'm just in a bad mood today, of course he didn't mean to forget your play.'

If you find out your ex has been breaking the rules find a time to talk to him or her. If the rule breaking is minor you could do it over the phone but I think it's better to meet face to face, out of earshot of the children, if there's either a major incident or he or she has been doing it persistently. Don't go in ready for a fight, because you'll get one, and your ex will concentrate of defending themselves rather than recognising the problem. Question first rather than accuse. Remember that it's irrelevant whether you're hurt or upset. The only reason to have this discussion is to provide good parenting for your children. Keep that in mind and the focus of what you say and it'll be difficult for your ex to argue. Ask your ex if they continue to agree that the rule is necessary. It's very likely that they forgot about the rule in the heat of a moment or didn't realise that their action constituted breaking the rule.

If this discussion doesn't work ultimately there is nothing you can do. The rules are there to stop arguments so don't make this into one. Don't try to punish you ex by restricting visits or maintenance payments or acting badly yourself. This is very likely to result in an escalation of ill feeling between the two or you. One person sticking to the rules is still better than neither of you sticking to them. It's irritating and unfair if your ex is now flouting them but children have eyes and ears; he or she really won't be doing themselves any favours with them. Bite your tongue and continue to set a good example by sticking to the rules yourself.

# Discipline

When children are young discipline can usually be resolved quickly and easily. The younger they are the more they'll benefit from consistent rules at both homes for things such as bedtimes and rules on watching the TV, etc. It's far better to soften one of your principles than have very different rules in each home. If there are some differences acknowledge them with the children but don't criticise the differences. The children will need to learn to accept that two households may have different rules just like there are different rules at school and at home (and perhaps even when they go to their grandparents').

As children get older discipline becomes more difficult. If things go really wrong then it's tempting to start to blame each other and it can easily cause arguments. But by far the best way of dealing with serious behavioural issues is as a united team. Teenagers will know you better than anyone else and will know exactly where your pressure points are. When there are two parents raising a teenager is extremely tough and emotionally draining. When you're a single parent the difficulties double because they'll make their rebellion far more personal. For example, if you've not managed to find new friends and a new partner they will tell you that you only want them to come home earlier because you're a 'frigid old cow with no social life'. If you have a good social life and a new boyfriend they'll tell you that you only want them to come home earlier because you're such a 'drunk/slag yourself' and you think they'll behave as badly as you do; you really can't win and they know all your guilty secrets to make this as painful as possible for you. As soon as you get your ex to stand by you and tell them that you both want them home by a certain time then it's far more difficult for them to attack you personally in response and they're much more likely to respect the rules you're both trying to enforce. They'll also feel much happier and more secure.

## Lea's story:

My daughter, Eve (although not normally a difficult child), went through a phase when she was 14 that I found really difficult to deal with. I was a 'depressed psycho' (she knew I'd been on antidepressants) if I so much as asked her to take her trainers upstairs. Everything I said was turned into an argument, however careful I was. I tried to convince myself that teenagers have raging hormones that cause them to act so badly and that it wasn't really her or me; but she made me question whether it was my mental state and I felt awful. It came to a head one night when she left the house at midnight after an argument. When she came home she phoned her father to tell him what an evil bitch I was. I overheard the call and spoke to him later. He backed me up completely. That made a massive difference, as she was no longer able to abuse me personally, as she had been, and had to question her behaviour. It also made me more confident in my dealings with her. Our relationship immediately improved and things started getting much better.

However about six months later, when Eve was at her father's, I got a call from him to say that Eve had disappeared. She was gone nearly 24 hours and her phone was switched off. She texted him once to say she was staying out but didn't wait to get permission. She eventually turned up at my house and I called her father, who, having imagined her dead, was in a very emotional state, which was very unlike him. We sat in my living room together to question her. Eve tried to lie her way out of trouble for a while. When that didn't work she told my ex that it was his fault because he gave his step-daughter more attention and love than he gave her. He burst into tears and hugged her, apologising. She'd obviously identified one of the issues he worried about, as she had with my depression. I was furious with her; it was clear that she was exploiting him just like she'd exploited me so I angrily told her how horrible her behaviour was and backed him up like he'd backed me up. After that neither of us really had any problems with Eve. She realised that she couldn't play us off against each other, or make things personal. She's a lovely girl now but I'm pretty sure that without us supporting each other during these crises things would not have turned out so well.

## Your new social life

Some mothers I spoke to didn't think it was right for them to have a social life, particularly if their children were very young, 'They need me too much. I wouldn't feel right going out partying until they're older' and, particularly in the early days after the separation, children do need a lot of time and care to rebuild their sense of security. However one side effect of divorce is that, if your ex does have the children for a reasonable length of time, you'll suddenly find you have free time that you haven't had since you were single. Many parents find this frightening. It's been cited to me by child counsellors as the real reason why many parents fight so hard to get custody of their children. These parents have defined themselves so much by their children and fulfilling their children's needs that without them they wander lost around an empty house mourning them, even if they only lose their children for part of the weekend. That's clearly unhealthy for you and your children. Children shouldn't be made to feel responsible for you and your happiness and you shouldn't make them worry about you when they're not with you, so it's time to rebuild your social life and start to do things just for you. That way, when they come back after they've spent time with your ex, you can all happily share stories without anyone feeling guilty.

While married you probably found that most of the people you mixed with were other couples who were parents of children of a similar age. This can change when you divorce. One reason for this is that you might feel you have less in common with them and, as you're not part of a couple any more, you don't quite fit like you used to. Don't be surprised if some of your friends now actively shun you. Some of these friends will see you a threat to them, either because they think you'll try and steal their spouse or because they think divorce is a contagious disease. That isn't as daft as it sounds. Many people know they have problems in their marriage but divorce is still a very big deal. It becomes less of a big deal if someone you respect does it, particularly if they don't seem too badly affected. Consequently it's not unusual for the divorce of one couple in a group to create a stampede to the divorce courts for the rest. The idea that you might steal their spouses is also based on fact. Single people over a certain age are available in far smaller numbers than when you were ten or more years younger, so men and women often first focus on their friends around them for a future partner. I know two women who are now married to the best men at their first weddings. So don't be too scathing of the friends who now want to distance you but try to reassure them as much as you can and hope that things can be repaired as soon as you're 'safely' paired up again.

This losing of some friendships will probably be balanced by you forming new friendships with others who've been divorced themselves and will welcome you to the 'club'. These friends may have children of similar ages to your own so it's very possible that these friendships will work for your children too as you can all offer support to each other.

The new friends that will fit less easily into your life, as a single but responsible parent, will be those who aren't parents and/or have never been married. These friends can be a welcome reminder of unencumbered single life and make you feel young again. However many have no idea of the responsibilities of being a parent or how to behave around children. Someone who is fun to go out partying with may have a disruptive influence if introduced to your children. They might, for example, be used to talking disparagingly about the opposite sex or how drunk they were and relate to your children either as other adults or as people who aren't really there, so will speak as if they won't be heard by them. They might also try to pull you away from your responsibilities, suggesting that you're overprotective and do too much for your children. As a general rule I only consider childcare advice, which conflicts with my own instincts, if it comes from parents of similar- or older-aged children. Some friends may even resent your relationship with your children, or the fact that your biological clock isn't ticking like theirs is.

### Kanta's story:

When I divorced my children were six and eight years old. I spent the first couple of years really enjoying my freedom. My ex would have them most weekends and I formed some great new friendships well away from what I now saw as the dull school mums who had nothing in their lives except getting the dinner ready on time.

One of my friends called Shriti was particularly lively and we had a good time together until she got tickets to go to the opening of a club. She hadn't checked with me first and the children were due to be with me on the date of the opening and not with their dad. I tried to get my ex to have them but he couldn't; he had some business trip he had to go on. I managed to get a babysitter but that meant I needed to be home by midnight (the girl who was coming was only 16 and doing exams soon). I explained the problem to Shriti but she wasn't very sympathetic and first suggested I should insist my ex take them and then that they were old enough to be left alone, particularly as they'd be asleep.

We went to the club but, of course, it only started to liven up at 11 pm, when I needed to think about leaving. Shriti had promised, reluctantly, that she would travel home with me because otherwise I wouldn't have gone, but when the time came she wouldn't leave and insisted I was being silly and overprotective, 'My mum left us alone all the time and we never came to any harm. You need to stop being so overprotective and enjoy yourself.' I couldn't get her to come with me so I had travel back by myself; which was difficult and expensive as I didn't want to go on the train at that time of night dressed like that and alone. Shriti and I had planned to get a cab but on my own the fare was much more than I could afford so I had to cut the shopping bill the following week to make up the budget. I felt so guilty.

Don't let these warnings put you off forming friendships with the single and childless. I have some fantastic single friends who've been an enormous help and support to me, particularly in overcoming the huge culture shock of being single in the noughties, having last been single in the 1970s. My two daughters have many things in common with these single friends that I don't, and my friends have picked up on issues that I wouldn't have spotted. The best are able to talk to them like a big sister would. Many of these friends have been far more effective at giving my children career aspirations than any official careers guidance by opening their eyes to what women can do and achieve.

## Sex as a single parent

Handling developing relationships is dealt with in the following chapter but before you settle down again you'll probably have some less significant relationships (or flings) that have slightly different considerations for children.

Do you really remember that horrible feeling of being 'available' which, for a single mother, seems to make men think that you're a sad case and fair game for anything? I don't believe it's any easier for men with the entrenched tradition that they have to take their ego in their hands and make the first approach. It's a bit like many painful parts of life; somehow you forget how bad it is until you're back there asking yourself why you're putting yourself through this again. The cattle market can be even worse this time as some people still have the attitude that, as a single mother (or father), you should be grateful for any attention you get.

Below are some particularly outrageous remarks that I, and some of my friends, have been subjected to. I've included them so you don't run down the nearest hole in depression when you get them:

- 'I can't understand why no one wants you.' I must have got this one at least once a week. Why do some people not realise how insulting it is to assume that single parents would happily accept anyone who wanted them and not realise that it's probably because you've not found anyone you want?
- 'You'll probably die a sad, lonely old woman.' This assumes that no one would want a single mother and, even worse, that being without a partner is the same as being sad and lonely.
- 'You're probably too choosy.' And being single is worse than being with someone who you don't want to be with?
- 'At your age you should be grateful for any man

you can get.' This was said to an attractive 35-year-old single mother.

- 'I'll sleep with you but I don't want to kiss you.'

But the prize for the worst chat-up line goes to:

- 'Are we going to have sex or what? I'm really not bothered either way.'
- And after one date, a few texts and a couple of telephone conversations, 'I want you to stop messing with me now; this has gone on long enough, when are we going to have sex?'

Don't let any stupid remarks diminish your self-esteem. Remember that you have a duty to yourself and to your children not to settle, as that'll simply lead to relationship upsets in the future. The world may have moved on, attitudes have changed, but you still have the right to lead your relationships at the pace and in the way that you're comfortable with. Remember that you're setting an example that your children will follow, either now or in the future. And you wouldn't want them to be bullied in this way, would you?

Dating again, when you have children, will be strongly reminiscent of when you were dating as a teenager and had to avoid being caught by your parents. Your children will be on the alert for someone new coming into their lives, someone who will have the right to boss them about, have a greater influence over you than they do and who'll move in and make changes. If you think about it from their perspective it's not too surprising that they're so interested. The first time a man came to pick me up I was shocked when I came home to receive the judgement from my daughters that he was not the man for me. On questioning, I discovered that they came to this conclusion because he was wearing the wrong coloured shirt. The absurdity of making a judgement on that basis was not the most curious aspect to it. Our house is laid out so you can't see anyone at the door except if you climb into the kitchen sink to see over the café-style curtain we have there. My daughters must have both done that in the few seconds it took for me to walk to his car.

The younger your children are the less likely they are to understand the pattern of adult relationships. When you start dating again you should therefore try to keep it from your children for as long as possible; particularly these first relationships, and if they do know that you're going out with someone make it clear that it's early days and they shouldn't jump to any conclusions about where the relationship will lead. If you're very excited about a new partner enthuse with your friends, not your children, as that early excitement may well fizzle out just as quickly as it came.

Even very early on in relationships some dates will start to voice their opinions on your children and how you raise them. It's a very useful indication of the sort of person they are. One friend told me, 'I was dating Ruth for two years and was always very generous towards her young children, including them in holidays and spending lots on them at Christmas. Despite this, one day she was really critical of me for spending the same amount on my own daughters, telling me I was being too generous.' I briefly dated a man myself who told me I should stop Stephanie playing football, a sport she excelled at and loved, because it was too masculine. Make sure you listen to these early warning signs.

Some divorcees become very sexually adventurous immediately after a divorce and that has to be handled sensitively. Keep overnight stays for when the children are with your ex for as long as you can. There should be no risk that your children meet new dates for the first time on the landing when they're both in a state of semi-undress or even worse find him/her naked in your bed doing strange animal impressions. I expect you don't ever want to be confronted with your children having sex (even when they're middle-aged and been married for 20 years); well, they'll feel the same way about you. For some reason the idea of our older and younger near relatives having sex is truly stomach churning. Teenagers also believe that old people (anyone over 25) shouldn't be interested in sex anyway.

## Kathy's story

I'd been divorced a couple of years and had only ever had men to stay when my teenage children were at their dad's. However one night my son was staying at his friend's and my daughter, Tina, had gone to bed early. My boyfriend, James, fell asleep cuddled up on the sofa and when he woke he clearly wanted more than a cuddle before he went home. As Tina had been in bed hours it seemed worth the risk and James set his watch alarm for 3 am so he could creep out of the house well before Tina was up.

What we didn't count on was quite how particular Tina was about her appearance. As James crept out of my room, just after 3 am, Tina was sitting on the tiny landing straightening her hair. He had to step right over her. I'm not sure who was the most embarrassed. I understand that they both very formally wished each other 'good morning'.

You also have to keep in mind that your children will believe that the moral rules you set yourself should apply to them. You can use this to your advantage, as it gives you a natural opener to sex education and related issues but if they know you have one-night stands you'll find it much more difficult to persuade them, once over 16, that they shouldn't do the same.

Just like some of us had parents who were blasé about our sex life to the point of embarrassing us, similarly some of us will be lucky or unlucky enough to have children like that. A friend of mine frequently worked from home and was meeting Ian, an elderly and very serious male business colleague, when her teenage daughter came home. Out of politeness, the girl was introduced to Ian and then, in front of her poor mother and Ian, she asked, 'So is Ian sleeping with you tonight? Why not? You don't need to be embarrassed just because I'm here. I know you would if I wasn't.' My friend started to panic that her daughter would actually offer them her condom stash but eventually managed to silence her daughter before a visibly shocked Ian was embarrassed any further.

## Coping with sole custody

Getting the father or mother of your children out of your life most or all of the time may seem like a victory at the time. If you do decide to, or are stuck with, raising your children alone you'll soon realise that it's a very challenging situation.

Children's emotional development does seem to be helped by having good role models representing both genders in their lives. You'll also probably find that discipline as a lone parent is much more difficult. Sometimes it's really helpful for your child and for you to be able to talk to another concerned adult.

It's therefore worth looking for an alternative adult figure to take an active role in your child's life. This person should be constant and preferably someone the child or children already respect and have a good relationship with. This will rule out new dates until they become a more permanent fixture in your life. Even if you've married again, or are in a permanent relationship, the tensions of step-relationships, particularly in the early days, might make them a barrier to resolving conflict rather than a help for some years. Instead look at the relationship your child, or children, has with their relatives, particularly grandparents or childless aunts and uncles. Some long-term family friends might also be able to fulfil this role. This adult should be willing to take on a more active role with your child and have a genuine interest and concern in their well-being. As well as helping you deal with crises, it's useful for this adult to be a frequent visitor to your home so the children feel that they can confide in them.

Having sole custody of a child is emotionally draining. You won't get the time away from your children to develop your social life and find time to do the things you want. Instead you'll probably find yourself investing all your time and energy in your children and start to find it difficult to see a life beyond them. This can feel like a sacrifice worth making unless it affects your happiness and general mood. Children will suffer from any unhappiness or bad temper that results from your discontent. It's therefore usually better for your children, as well as yourself, that you find time to enjoy yourself away from them on a regular basis. A parent who's happy and content but has a few hours a week away from the responsibilities of being a parent is usually better able to make the children feel 'wanted' than a parent who never leaves his or her children and is bogged down with the stress of it. This doesn't mean you become a party animal with the social life of a single person.

Try to find friends in a similar position to yourself so that you can help each other out, at no charge, with babysitting and other emotional support. If you find it difficult to find these friends use every opportunity you can when you're out and about. If you see a mother struggling with children help her out; it may be the start of a great friendship; start talking to other parents at the activities your children attend and invite other children to your house to play with yours as it gives you a very good opener with the parents. If all these daily activities don't result in some mutually supportive new friends then the internet and newspapers can now be used to find friends in exactly the same way as you can find dates.

You'll have a lot to get through every day, particularly if you're working as well as being a lone parent. Unless you actually enjoy housework and feel uncomfortable if your home isn't immaculate, go easy on the chores and ditch or reduce the frequency wherever you can. One of my favourite sayings is 'An immaculate home is the sign of a wasted life' and unironed sheets and a light sprinkling of dust are less important than children feeling loved and their parent being happy.

## Becoming a time lord

The most important thing you can give your children is your time. Unless you spend time with them, it's unlikely that you'll find out if they have any worries that might affect them for the rest of their lives. You need to know what's on their minds and who their friends are and that means lots of conversations with as few distractions as possible. It's very easy to let this go when life gets busy. Each time it's happened to us I've noticed an immediate deterioration in my relationship with my children and their behaviour and I then needed to work extra hard to get it back on track.

When I was a child family dinners were the time when everyone sat down together without distractions. As a working mother, I find it a challenge to get the family together like that. If I'm in London I get home too late and at weekends everyone seems to go out at different times so unless I grab every opportunity or book it into their diaries, it simply doesn't happen. Both my daughters used to resist it, making the usual excuses such as telling me that they wanted to watch something on TV (I deliberately don't have one in the kitchen where we eat) or that they need to eat earlier. But now I think they actually recognise the benefits. If we're struggling in our relationship, or I'm really concerned about something, I take them out for dinner. It doesn't need to be expensive (the local fast-food joint is fine) but if you're sitting at a table in a restaurant together the focus can only be on each other, not on what programme is coming on TV. The other advantage of going out is that no one can lose their temper (it's too public) and you can risk the conversation moving around more naturally without the danger that you'll lose the chance to get back to what you really need to talk about. It's also difficult for children to feel offended by this approach. Instead they recognise that it's not about you 'getting' at them; it's much clearer that you want the chance to sit down and really understand what's going wrong. Of course some subjects are not appropriate for restaurants so it doesn't work for really deep personal chats.

Unfortunately my daughters cottoned on to the reason I took them out for dinner pretty quickly and if I suggested it they looked at me with guilty concern at what they'd done wrong. The result is that, whereas I'm pretty confident that neither of them is scarred by the divorce, I have a nagging worry that they'll spend the rest of their lives mentally connecting eating out with deep uncomfortable conversations. Of course you'll realise that the way to avoid this is to make sure you take your children out for dinner on plenty of other occasions.

With younger children outings can achieve a similar effect. These don't have to be expensive. A walk out in the park where the two of you can chat about things that matter to them can completely change a child's mood. Sunday mornings cuddled up in your bed can be really lovely at any age, even when they're really big, if they surface in time. If you have more than one child try and give them each some one-on-one time with you. If you're so busy that it's difficult to fit this in try combining it with other things you have to do such as asking them to take turns in helping you get a job done. As they'll love having you to themselves, you may find that you get more offers of help than you would otherwise expect. Instead of shouting at teenagers to tidy their room, offer to do it with them; this will make it into a bonding session rather than another chance for the two of you to fall out; but don't force it, as some teenagers like to keep their rooms very private (possibly with very good reason).

Homework is another chance for you to have valuable one-on-one time with them. It's usually distracting if you try talking to them about what else is going on in their lives, but it is just a chance for you to be together.

With time so scarce for divorced parents, you need to be really creative in how you find it and continually reassess where the opportunities are. Always make sure you all enjoy it and look forward to it. It shouldn't be a chore. Most recently Stephanie became a fitness consultant at a gym which Gabriella also joined. I hated the idea of going to the gym; I could think of better ways of using up my energy, but I saw it as a chance for us all to spend time with each other in a natural unforced way. Gabriella and I started going together, which helped our relationship, and Stephanie got a chance to show off her professional skills. As a by-product of this bonding I lost a stone (14 pounds); that would be the one that I put on during the more stressful teenage years when we kept having to go out for dinner.

## Making them feel loved

All children need constant reminders that they still matter. It's very easy to think that older children don't need it but in my experience teenagers need it more than anyone. Don't give in to all their demands for things and for you to do stuff for them but do surprise them occasionally if you can. Buy that bag they raved about even though (and especially) if they've not nagged you for it, clear their room out for them or cook them a favourite meal when they're least expecting it. The key for this to work is that it's not something they expect; instead they'll recognise that you've put extra effort into making their lives better. It's a little but important way of underlining that you're thinking about them and know what's important to them. Even the odd 'love you lots' text message can make all the difference to their perception of their importance in your life and how much you really care about them. The child that knows that they're loved and valued is less likely to be unhappy or be persistently badly behaved.

It is really important that children feel comfortable in the new home. Things that you may think are unimportant could play a critical part in this so you do need to listen to them and ask open questions. This is not the time to tease them about their foibles. If the only way they'll be happy is if their bed faces the wall then try to accommodate that. Try and involve them in how their new rooms will look and, if you possibly can, make their rooms even more special than their old ones. This doesn't need to cost you extra; it may just mean burying your own tastes and pandering to theirs. If your daughter always wanted her room to be pink and fluffy then let her have it. Discussing how they want their new room decorated can take their mind off the negative aspect of divorce and on to the more exciting one.

However much you love them, at times you may find yourself resenting your children. Unfortunately it's difficult to hide this from them and your children won't feel loved if they think they're making you unhappy. They may even believe it, even if it's not true. Being a martyr to your children therefore really doesn't work. Ultimately it can, and often does, lead to clinical depression so go easy on yourself; don't try and do everything, focus on what's important to you and your children and give yourself time to find out who you are and what you want. If you're finding that something is too much by yourself address the problem before your resentment builds up. Don't be afraid of letting your children know that you're human and have not been born to serve them. 'I can't take you ice skating on Saturday because I've already got plans myself' does not make you a bad parent, by contrast a parent who always drops everything for their children is teaching children to assume that everyone else's plans come second to theirs. Children who believe that tend to grow up to be inconsiderate, as they've never been taught that they need to consider the needs of others. Being selfish occasionally and putting your needs first will certainly do no damage and if it stops your children feeling resented then everyone will be much happier.

Don't try to be supermum or dad. I'm sure my children would give me ticks as well as black marks for my mothering skills but I've tried to ensure that they continue to feel safe (appropriate to their age), that the structure and support is there in their lives and that they don't feel they have to fend for themselves in a chaotic home. That's much more important than being a 24/7 chef and chauffeur or having a bottomless purse.

# CHAPTER 6

## ESTABLISHING A NEW FAMILY

- The one-parent family
- Forming new relationships
- Marriage or moving in together
- Step-parents
- Step-siblings
- Christmas and other social minefields

You'll probably find that your life starts to settle down again more quickly than you would have expected and you'll soon establish yourselves as a new family unit. Whether this is with or without a new partner, you need to be aware of the shape it's taking as you can find yourself slipping into roles that store up problems for the future.

# The one-parent family

One-parent families have such an appalling press that the phrase now almost sounds like a swear word. However unless your ex has disappeared, your children still have two parents to raise them. There are obvious financial and practical issues but the advice I've given you so far should now start to pay dividends and make them much easier to handle. You should, for example, now be able to do what you want for entire weekends, whether that's watching the TV programmes or taking part in the sports you've had to miss since you became a parent. The lovely thing is that instead of feeling overburdened with the pressure of looking after your children, like the single parents who've 'won' sole custody, you'll genuinely look forward to seeing your children again and listening to their news. They'll gain from the more relaxed person you'll become as well as the security of having two parents to love and look out for them, just like the children in an 'intact' family.

There are, however, some things to warn you about in your new household. You may find that without another adult in the home you begin to let your children fulfil this role. You'll start to confide in them, sharing your worries and giving them added responsibilities; it feels almost natural to fill the adult vacancy with your children. Whether you do that or not, it's quite common for children to start to take on adult roles in one-parent households. With boys in their mother's care, this can typically make them assume the role of head of the household (I know you didn't give them that title but they can assume it even if they've only just been potty trained). Girls can become very protective of both their mothers and fathers and with their father, they can take on the role of 'mother' with their younger siblings.

There are two problems with taking this too far. Firstly children aren't emotionally equipped to take on the burden of adult worries. They don't have control over their lives like an adult does so there is usually little they can do to help the situation, only worry about it, often long after the problem has been resolved. And it's when people are burdened with worries, but helpless to do anything about them, that they're most likely to feel stressed.

You're not your child's best friend, you're their parent. There's a big difference. Parents are there to support children and listen to their worries but not the other way round. So it's OK to discuss minor issues that are worrying you but avoid making them your confidant in the way you would an adult. Studies have shown that many parents place this huge unfair burden on their children after divorce and this has a long-term negative affect on the children.

### Mark's story:

My ex-wife treated our daughter, then 16, more like a friend than a daughter. They used to go clubbing together, get drunk together, stay out all night and even passed on boyfriends to each other. My daughter thought this was great at the time. I was the one who had to be the nasty one; insisting that when she was with me that she was home on school nights, that she didn't drink in places under age and that she dressed appropriately. Of course at the time she hated me, but that's part of being a parent; they're going to hate you sometimes.

She's now 22 and much closer to me than to her mum. She told me recently that she doesn't feel she has a mum. She recognises now that her mother encouraged her to act irresponsibly instead of protecting her from her own teenage stupidity and now she doesn't see her as someone who can guide and support her. Her mum is just like another friend, a good friend, but not a mother.

The second problem with treating your children as your adult confidant and friend is that it will make it very difficult for your children to ever accept you having a new partner, because that person will not be filling a vacancy but will be usurping your child's role as the other 'adult' in your life. The new partner, and you, will most likely try and return the children to their normal role in the family unit but because of the privileges they've experienced this will be hugely resented, making it far more difficult to get the step-relationship to work. Girls will feel competitive with a new woman in the house and boys will bitterly resent someone taking over their role as 'head of the household'.

### Angela's story:

My mum left us when I was 10. Dad was devastated and he spent most of the first few months just watching TV. He didn't eat properly and he rarely seemed to wash or shave. I had a younger brother, Ben, who was six. Someone had to make sure that he was fed and had stuff for school and so I soon found myself doing most of the housework and cooking. As Dad came out of his depression, he seemed to appreciate it but never really questioned it, which as an adult I find pretty bizarre as I was so young. We all got on fine though until Dad brought this new woman back; I always referred to her as 'the old bitch' and I can't remember her name now.

The very first time she came to the house she made comments about the house 'clearly needing a woman's touch' which I really resented and on her second visit she started rearranging stuff in my cupboards. She'd affectionately ruffle my father's hair and tell him how he 'needed looking after'; she'd correct what I was doing and tell me I was sweet for 'trying to help' and would then get a duster out herself to 'get the place in some sort of order'. I wanted to thump her; instead when I made her tea I spat in it. She drank it and told me she'd teach me 'how to make tea properly'.

It still annoys me when I think about the way she thought she could just storm into our lives, take over and undermine everything I'd done. I did everything I could to drive that relationship apart. Eventually I succeeded. She volunteered to collect Ben from somewhere and I made sure she was given the wrong time so that poor Ben was left stranded by the road for an hour in tears. Dad had experienced how reliable I was (I'd always been there for him) so when she left Ben stranded, while she was at the hairdressers, he believed it was her being irresponsible. He was furious and we never saw her again. Poor Dad only started dating again when we'd both left home and he told me recently that he didn't want his love life to put the children who'd cared for him in any jeopardy. When he said that I felt very guilty but I wasn't brave enough to tell him that 'the old bitch' had actually told him the truth.

# Forming new relationships

One of the upsets many children of divorced parents have to endure is a long procession of unsuitable adults parading disturbingly through their life, or their parents jumping straight into another relationship that's scarcely any better, if not worse, than the one that they left (and so is likely to break up). This is often because, contrary to expectations, most people find that being single again, after a relationship and marriage that's lasted any length of time, can be pretty scary so it's very tempting to grab hold of the first exit from that state that you can find.

Unless someone comes along who completely bowls you over, and you're absolutely sure that its not to avoid being alone, give yourself a few months to build your self-confidence as a single person and discover who you are, what you want out of life and therefore who you really want to share it with. In a relationship your sense of self is often strongly influenced by feedback from your partner and towards the end of a marriage, and during a break-up, that's usually negative. Give yourself time and concentrate instead on making your children feel secure again. That way any new relationship will be formed because you want that person in your life not because you need someone to cling on to.

My mother told me that at first it really upset her whenever one of us children (there were four of us) split up with a boyfriend or girlfriend. One day the person was like another member of the family, in and out the house all the time, and the next they were gone for ever, without even the chance to say goodbye. Eventually she learned not to get attached to these passing partners and has advised me to do the same with my daughters' dates. Your children, particularly if they're young, are unlikely to be able to keep themselves so detached, so you should carefully manage how attached they're allowed to get to your new partners. Teenagers are more likely to understand the transient nature of relationships so you probably don't need to be as careful. You can manage how attached your children get to your dates by restricting visits to your home and involvement in their lives until the relationship is serious and be careful what you say about him or her to them so that you don't raise false expectations. If you do then break up from a relationship where an attachment has been formed, even if it was short and didn't mean much to you, you need to consider carefully how it will affect your children in the same way you did when you separated from their father. Just because your children have no blood relationship with your ex-boyfriend or ex-girlfriend you shouldn't assume that their departure from your life won't affect them. The story below is a very common one.

### Tess's story:

My mother dated Greg for four years from when I was three to when I was seven. He was lovely to my brother and me, giving us far more love and attention than our dad ever did. When my mum had no money, which was most of the time, he made sure we had what we needed. I can even remember him buying my first school uniform after Dad had refused to give Mum the money she needed for it. He didn't live with us but he stayed over twice a week and always on Saturday night. I used to look forward to seeing Greg on Sunday morning. We all had Sunday dinner together and it's one of the happiest memories of my childhood, as it was the one time we felt like a 'proper' family.

One Sunday morning I burst into Mum's room, really excited to see Greg and tell him all my news and Greg wasn't there. He and Mum had split and Mum had a new boyfriend. My brother and I were devastated but that seemed irrelevant to Mum. He was the best dad I ever had but because he was just one of, what turned out to be, many boyfriends he just disappeared from our lives one day and that was that.

Children can be a hurdle when you're trying to find someone new in your life. Some potential partners will make it clear to you that they only want you and not your 'baggage'. At least that's honest: because others will only make that view clear by their attitude to your children when they have to deal with them. To avoid any misunderstandings, find out as early as possible. Don't lie when you're asked by a new date; let it be known from the outset and see their reaction (unless you're just looking for a fling that won't be introduced to your children). Although children are 'baggage' to a relationship some potential dates will actually welcome the fact you have children. To use myself as an example, I'm a middle-aged mother, still of childbearing age, and a man without children is not a particularly attractive long-term option for me. He'll either want children, so I'll have to start it all again (which many parents will understand is a bit like coming to the end of a marathon and being told you have to run it again) or he doesn't have children because he doesn't like them, which doesn't suggest great stepdad potential. The only positive alternative is if he's infertile, but that's not a question I normally like to ask a man before I've even been out on a date with him. Men have told me that they're put off by the urgency of the biological clock ticking in women over 30 so with mothers they find that they can have a less pressurised relationship. Therefore whatever gender you are you shouldn't assume that having children will put potential dates off.

It's very easy, when trying to find a new partner, to forget romance and instead find someone who would be good for your children and quickly re-establish the comfortable family life you miss. Jane told me, 'I went out with a man for a while who was fantastic with the children plus he had lots of money. I seriously considered marrying him for the sake of my children. I love them and I wanted to take their hurt away and give us a good lifestyle again and this seemed like the perfect opportunity. The trouble was I didn't fancy him and wasn't in love with him, but that seemed selfish in the bigger picture of how good he'd be for us.' As Jane realised in time, the danger with this is that you're setting yourself up for another divorce. Yes, you need to consider whether a new partner will be a good parent for your children but that should be considered alongside your own needs, for everyone's sake.

When you do find a significant new partner it's a good idea to let your children get to know them slowly before there is even talk of them moving in with you. Make this informal and relaxed; so hanging around watching TV, while they wait for you to get ready to start with would be the sort of thing I mean, rather than big formal family dinners. Your new partner should not assume any parental role until they're well established in the family unit.

## Craig's story:

I was brought up by just my mum from the age of about seven. For the first few years it was just us and then she started dating again. At first I was pleased but then this man, Tony, came to the house and sat in my dad's old chair and alarm bells went off in my head. He was nice to me to begin with and bought me presents and, although they were usually either too young or too old for me, I recognised even then that he was making an effort with me. However Tony's visits became more frequent and he started staying overnight. The first time it happened I naïvely believed that it was simply because it was too late for him to go home. Then one of my mates made some crack about my mum getting 'a seeing to' and I realised what was happening and was pretty disgusted that anyone could behave like that towards my mum.

Tony slowly started to assume a role in the house. At first it was just fixing things and then he began to make suggestions about how much TV I should be allowed to watch and the time I should go to bed. I even heard him telling my mum that she was too soft on me and that I'd grow up to be a 'sissy' unless she allowed him to teach me how to be a 'man' which seemed to mean I should be taken to football, even though he knew I found it boring, and that I should stick up to the bullies at school without complaining to her (these guys carried knives!). By this time I was about 13 and it was clear that they were thinking of moving in together. I became the kid from hell. I hated this man for violating my mother, taking over my home and for thinking he could tell me what to do.

It came to a head one day when he came round when my mum was out. I was sitting doing my homework on the kitchen table, drinking a beer. He had a real go at me for drinking alcohol. I told him to get lost (in more offensive language than that) and how I was only doing what he'd told me to do and being more 'manly'. As far as I was concerned he had no right to have a go at me for drinking beer from my own fridge in my own home. I think it was the excuse he needed to really have a go at me and we ended up physically fighting. He wasn't a big guy and I was pretty well developed for my age so it was pretty even.

After that there was no way that my mum could get us to accept each other: it was all out war between us. I told her that if she wanted that nasty piece of scum mauling her in preference to her own son that I would leave and find my dad. She ditched Tony.

As a parent yourself, you probably know that adults are usually more protective and more proud of their children than anything else in their lives, so getting them on side is actually a pretty good idea if you want to impress your lover or prospective lover. Many adults will therefore bend over backwards, sideways and do double back somersaults if necessary to get the object of their affection's children on side when they first arrive on the scene. Children will usually be far more astute about the games being played than the love-struck adults around them but most cannily figure that having suffered the divorce it's now payback time. If this virtual stranger that Mummy or Daddy seems to be spending a lot of time with wants to throw money at them, who are they to argue?

One 15-year-old girl told me about her father's new girl-friend: 'If she thinks she can bribe me into liking her by buying me an annual pass to all the theme parks... she'd be dead right.' Some would worry that it was using the children, setting false expectations or spoiling them but it can get the relationship off to a good start and, although children will see through the behaviour, they appreciate the effort; as this girl explained, it 'showed willing'.

If you play this type of game I think the real danger is that your own children will be jealous, particularly if you're significantly more generous than you normally are with them. Children talk, so don't assume that the fact you bought your new partner's daughter an expensive present, or paid for her to go on holiday, won't get back to your own children. Your children will not appreciate your need to ingratiate yourself with some kids you've just met, just to get some woman or man, who they don't want in their lives anyway, to like you. They know how generous you normally are and any deviation from that to these virtual strangers will set off jealousies before you've even reached the first hurdle of stepfamily life.

You need to handle your sex life with your new partner just as carefully as I advised you to handle more transient lovers. You may think that sex is a private thing of no concern to your children, but unfortunately you'll find that it can create problems in the family. Children don't like to see their parents as sexual beings, even if you're married. In the 'intact' family this doesn't present too much of a problem, as by the time the children are aware of sex, typically the parents are way past the lust stage and instead feel a sense of pride if they manage to count their encounters in double figures over the course of a year. You might have forgotten all about the 'can't keep our hands off each other stage' but in a new relationship it's likely to reappear. The children will have to accept some degree of affection between you but it's rude to shove it in their faces; remember how you feel when you have to watch people indulging in PDAs (public displays of affection) and try to imagine how you'd feel if you could hear your children or your parents at it (OK, they may be even more wrinkled than you are but the yuck score will be the same for your children).

For the same reason, avoid leaving things around that boasts of your new sexual relationship. Whips, maid outfits and handcuffs tend to have particularly high 'yuck' scores, as can one of you being particularly noisy in the throes of passion. If all this sounds light-hearted, it can be, but keep in mind that this is not a trivial subject. Some children can get disturbed by it, particularly if they're too young to understand that you're not actually hurting each other.

### Mo's story:

My dad and his new girlfriend were really loud and even left their door open a couple of times. I was 11 but it really embarrassed and frightened me. I used to phone my mum up and plead with her to collect me. My poor mum had to ask my dad if he could be a little more 'discreet' about it and of course they then got into a slanging match about her being jealous because his new girlfriend wasn't frigid like she was. I could have told him, from the stuff she and her new man left 'lying' around the locked cupboard in her bedroom, that she wasn't frigid any more, but I didn't think either of them would appreciate that bit of insight.

The really funny thing is that when I got married we had to spend our wedding night with my dad and stepmum (as she was by then), as it was on the way to the airport and we had an early flight. When we arrived I discovered they'd put us in separate rooms. When I challenged him my father told me it would embarrass everyone if we stayed in the same room. I reminded him what he'd put me through as a child and how hypocritical he was being and I found out then that he honestly thought it was just my mother stirring things up and hadn't understood how I could find it disturbing.

These experiences can also bind step-siblings together as they all agree how disgusting their parents are. Maya told me, 'My stepsister and I were pretty cold towards each other until one night our parents went to bed "early" and we could both hear them at it. It was *so* gross that we both rushed to put our headphones in and started to giggle.'

The start of a new relationship is one of the times when you'll be thanking me for persuading you to bite your tongue off to keep on good terms with your ex, as the shared care will give you the valuable alone time your new relationship needs. The time you do have your children around, and have to be more restrained, will probably help keep things exciting for longer. We all want what's forbidden far more than what's on a plate every day. Just try to avoid packing your children's stuff too eagerly when it's time for them to move. If the children are old enough, and you live close enough, I also suggest that you get them to check with you before dropping in to collect stuff that they've forgotten (they always forget things). The danger during this period is that they'll walk in when you're taking advantage of the empty house and refuse to eat at the kitchen table ever again.

I warned you in Chapter 4 that even if your ex left you for someone else you forming a new relationship can raise jealousy and ill feeling and make your ex less cooperative and amicable than they had been. You need to remember that when you introduce your ex to your new partner. One child told her counsellor, 'Dad keeps asking me if mum has another boyfriend. I don't know and I don't care. I wish they would stop going on about it. Why can't they just get back together – it was OK before?' And Cathy told me, 'My ex and I split, at his instigation, eight years ago and he's been married to someone else for the last six years, yet when he accidentally met my new boyfriend he went into a sulk.'

Stepfamilies that form immediately from the break-up will experience different problems to those that formed after the one-parent family was established. The main problem you're likely to have is the blame attached to the new partner, as the children will believe that without this person their parents would have stayed happily together. They may make a very deliberate effort to break you up. One way to get over this is to leave a few weeks (preferably months) between the separation and moving in with your new partner. That way your children can get used to things in stages rather than having to cope with both the separation and the new partner all at once.

If you've left your spouse for a homosexual relationship you'll need to handle it especially carefully. Emphasising that you've got nothing to be ashamed of will not win you the acceptance you need to go forward to form a loving family relationship. It's worth seeking the advice of support organisations and on the internet from people who've been through this. Many children are now less homophobic than adults, and may even think it's cool: it will partly depend how much exposure they've had to different ways of living. However you need to be prepared for your children to find it so embarrassing that they initially reject you. You have three major problems in gaining their acceptance. Firstly they'll think that the marriage must have been a lie so it disturbs their whole attitude to their childhood. Secondly children, particularly teenagers, like to disappear into the crowd and be the same as their friends, and this will mark them out. Finally, and probably the biggest hurdle you have, is that children usually like to think of their parents as sexless beings who form partnerships with adults for companionship only. Most of them know they're probably kidding themselves but that doesn't stop them holding on to that fantasy. Your children will probably recognise that you've had to overcome huge social pressures to publicly enter a gay relationship and you would not have done that if it was not about your sexual preference. Consequently they (like many adults) may have problems focusing beyond the sexual act to the loving relationship at the centre of it.

## Marriage or moving in together

Deciding to get married again should be considered very carefully. I warned you earlier about the need to handle how attached your children get to your new partners. When a partner is moving in, and becoming an important part of their lives, you'll be actively promoting that attachment. You'll want your children to form a bond with your new spouse and grow to accept their new family, including siblings, grandparents, etc. This success means that if it doesn't work out you'll have to put them through the trauma of divorce again. This second break-up can be worse for children than the first. Without the blood relationship, the new family's position in their lives does not have any obvious basis for continuing so these people, that you've encouraged them to love and consider as family, will probably disappear from their lives. That's a very tough blow for children.

Make sure you understand your new partner's attitude to your children before they move in. Do they know how often the children live with you? What's their attitude to that? Listen to any casual comments they make about your children, as that should give you an indication of whether you have a similar attitude to how children should be raised, but don't assume anything. If your new partner doesn't have children of their own they may not appreciate the sacrifices that go with being a parent; give them an opportunity to find out before they move in, such as going on a family holiday.

If your new partner does have children give them all a chance to get to know each other before you move in together, particularly if they're going to have to share a room. Try to have whole family weekends where everyone can hang out together and do their own thing. How the children will interact with each other will obviously largely depend on their genders and whether they're of a similar age. Intervening will make little difference (and is more likely to make things worse); you will need to give them all a chance to form their own relationships.

Do your children like your partner? Listen to what your children say about him or her. They probably know you very well and I've always found that my children's comments, though often very harsh, are well worth hearing. However you do need to be aware that some children will hate any new partner you have simply because they don't want anyone to replace their mother or father in your life.

Be as careful about telling your children that you're getting married again, or your partner is moving in with you, as you were when you told them you were getting divorced. Involve them in the wedding preparations and let them know what role you want them to play but don't expect them to be happy and excited by it.

# Step-parents

## The issues from the child's viewpoint

A step-parent is not the same as a parent. Eventually, if things go really well, they may start to assume aspects of that role and form a really good loving relationship. The mistake people make is to believe that someone new can join a family and immediately expect to be accepted enough to lay down the law; things need to be taken step by step. If you try to take things too quickly your children are likely to become very resentful.

Many children are instinctively frightened of a new adult in their mother or father's life. The traditional fairy tales with their stories of wicked step-parents don't help but they do have some basis in fact. Abuse and even murder of children is most commonly carried out by step-parents; so don't dismiss their fears, be proactive in reassuring them.

Jealousy is one of the most common reactions from children to a parent having a new significant other. This will be made worse if your children believe that the step-parent has broken up their parents or if they've had their parent to themselves for some time. They will then see the step-parent as the person who's breaking up the cosy relationship they have with their parent. You also need to be aware that it's very common for children to believe that the step-parent represents a barrier to their parents getting back together. They'll then believe it's in their interest to get rid of the newcomer as soon as possible. This happens even where the parents have been separated for some years.

You cannot force your children to love or even like their new step-parent; nor should you take it for granted that your children will want to spend time with them. Just because you've formed a new family, don't assume that the new family bonds will spring up any time soon, if ever. The more you push it the more your children will pull away from it. Your new partner is likely to be seen as an unwelcome interloper in their lives and your job is to show them that this is not someone who's taking you away from them. If you only ever see your children with your new partner (and stepchildren) then that's exactly what you're telling your children because, from their point of view, they never have private family time with you. How would you feel if you only ever got to see your best friend when they were with their new friends that you don't like much; friends that they're with when they're not with you? If you can show your children that your new life still leaves time for the special relationship you have with them then you'll start to win the battle of getting them to at least accept your new partner. In time you may then be able to act as a family. One child represented the views of many children when she told her counsellor, 'I got on really well with Dad when it was just me and him. Since *she* came along, he has no time for me.'

Many step-parents, in trying to assert their new position, will effectively act as a barrier between the children and their parent, causing huge resentment.

Here are some examples I've been given by adults and children of step-parent behaviour:

- The new stepmother demanding that her partner's teenage children call her 'mum' or refuse to let them see their father again (within six months of the father leaving the mother after an adulterous affair with her).
- Forbidding the children from contacting their father except through her ('So you don't hassle him too much; he's got a lot on at the moment.').
- Forbidding children from cuddling their father, or sitting on his lap, on the grounds that they're too old for that sort of behaviour (at eight years old).
- Hiding extra Christmas presents for their own children which the stepchildren found out about because their stepsister boasted about them.

These are all real examples that have happened in the past ten years. The first came from the child concerned (now an adult) but the stepmother explained to me at the time, 'I'm a good person. I don't see why I've been made out to be the baddie. I just wanted them to show me that they accept me and you have to start as you mean to go on.' None of the parents concerned are bad people, and in many ways made thoughtful and intelligent parents, but their one thoughtless action or comment caused huge damage. If you have problems do check that one or both of you hasn't behaved in a way, or said something, that I could include in this horrifying list.

Confidences between children and parents should stay that way; don't assume you can share them with the step-parent.

In your children's eyes that's another way of showing that your new spouse is getting in the way of your relationship with them.

The new family will need to agree the rules of the house and the natural parent should encourage the children to treat the step-parent with consideration. However it's important to understand that a step-parent will not have the same authority as the parent. Discipline, except where there is an immediate need, should be left to the natural parent until there is some affection and respect built up between the step-parent and the children. The discipline I find works best with children is where they know it comes with a huge dose of love attached. When they believe that love is there children usually want to please and don't want to let you down or upset you. With a step-parent, the children are more likely to see any discipline as an attempt by the 'usurper' to boss them around and will be met with something on the lines of the classic, 'You're not my real dad. You can't tell me what to do.' They may actively want to upset you; that may be the very reason why they're behaving badly.

As a parent yourself, you may think you understand children. However in my experience parents of only girls, and parents of only boys, do not have a good understanding of the issues in raising the other gender and you need to be aware of this. Teenage girls, for example, are often very shy of their own bodies and are embarrassed at being confronted by images of nudity or sexually explicit material or conversation (even where it is very mild references or artistic nudity). They simply haven't learned how to feel comfortable with their own sexuality. This is a normal developmental stage that most girls go through, and should be respected. I went through it, my daughters went through it and none of us would now be described as 'repressed'. Where a father with just sons takes on a stepdaughter with his new partner, or even a father with a daughter joins a family of sons, this may mean a change in behaviour to accommodate this sensitivity. Boys who've walked round the house will little on, displayed posters of semi-naked women and openly discussed their latest sexual conquests should be prevented from behaving like that in front of any new girls in the family. Privacy should be respected with locks on bathroom doors and a rule of knocking before entering the girl's bedroom. Sadly my experience is that the embarrassment the girl feels is mocked rather than respected which makes the feelings worse. These girls will then be very uncomfortable and go to huge lengths to avoid spending time in that household.

## The issues from the step-parent's viewpoint

Taking on someone else's children is not easy, even if you love children. There is nearly always a special bond with your own children and they grow up according to your rules and standards. Most parents love their children with a selfless instinctive strength that can be shocking in its intensity. Nature creates these bonds to enable us to deal with the fact that children are born incontinent, selfish and uncivilised (not the most romantic view, I know) but they are from our genes so nature tells us that it's even more important to protect them than to protect ourselves. Even as an adoptive parent, we can watch them grow from helpless lumps of flesh and take huge pride in all their achievements. When you take on someone else's children none of this applies. In fact the opposite is true; our natural instincts, as shown in many animals (such as lions), are to see the pre-existing offspring of our lover as threats to be extinguished.

If both of you have children that will be living with you at least part of the time then you and your new partner will probably be facing very similar challenges. However if one of you is childless then things will be much more difficult and you should tread with real care. We all think we know how children should be raised but the reality often makes us quickly ditch our prejudices. One woman I spoke to confessed, after a few glasses of wine, 'When I met Mike and we started our affair I saw his wife and children as little more than an inconvenience. He didn't love his wife and soon left her for me, which is how I thought it should be. I threw myself into play-acting the role of part-time "mother", bringing with me my naïve prejudices about how children should be brought up and was pretty damning on how their mother did things. It's was not until I had my own children, and I saw how precious the family bond is, that I realised what an ignorant cow I'd been. I would be devastated if someone took my children's father away from them and I think I would get quite violent if that woman was also childless and thought she knew better than me how my children should be raised.'

When you marry again remember that your new partner is marrying you and that the children are, at best, accepted as part of the package but it's the part of the package that, if they're really honest, they would probably have preferred to have done without. In the early stages of a relationship adults know that a good way to someone's heart is to be enthusiastic about their children. Parents are often so proud of their children and blinkered to their faults that he or she continues to assume that their partner, like their ex, loves the children and is happy to take on exactly the same parenting role. But once the day-to-day grind of caring for children becomes a reality it's very common for feelings to change very dramatically, yet still most step-parents are embarrassed to say what they really think.

In the same way that you shouldn't assume that your children will love their step-parent, who is nothing to them, until you've worked hard for the relationship to grow, your children are nothing to your new partner or your ex's new partner. Your children are a reminder to your new partner that you had a sexual relationship with someone prior to them. They are a drain on your joint resources and they often prevent couples having a honeymoon period in the relationship, as expected by people without children. People can go from being single and carefree to, overnight, having all the responsibilities of children without any of the excitement or choice in the matter. If your children are much younger than your new partner's children they may make them feel like they're going backwards in life. They've completed the stage your children are at and now have to go through it again. It's really common for children to resent the step-parent and work actively to make their lives miserable so that they'll end the relationship and, in the children's eyes, leave their natural parents free to marry each other again. They can be quite sneaky about this.

Why worry about how the step-parent is feeling in a book that is solely concerned with making divorce no big deal for children? I said in the introduction that the long-term interests of the children should not mean sacrificing the needs of the adults, as that too is detrimental to children. If you make the assumption that your new partner loves your children and is as happy to care for them and make sacrifices for them, as you are, then you're setting your children up for a miserable time. A tense unhappy step-parent will make the home life of your children stressful and possibly abusive and ultimately the pressure on the relationship will break it and lead to another divorce.

The lessons on step-parents from both the viewpoint of the child and that of the adult are actually very similar. They both put up with each other for your sake. It will take time for their relationship to grow and they may never do more than tolerate each other. Assuming they love each other like an 'intact' family does will cause resentment and problems that will put huge strains on everyone and have the potential to blast the new family apart. Both your children and your new partner need one-to-one time with you. Your children don't want your partner always around when you see them and your partner will want time for you two to have a proper relationship. Eventually, with lots of work from everyone, bonds will hopefully grow but wait for them, don't force them or assume they're there from the start.

## Dealing with your children's stepmother or stepfather

In addition to being a step-parent you may also have to 'deal' with your children having a step-parent. Essentially you should treat them much like you do your ex and put aside any personal squabbles you have. If you're still alone yourself it can feel like you've been replaced and that this person has effectively taken your family. It can be difficult looking at family photos of holidays they've all shared and not feel upset that they appear to be a normal happy family without you. That jealousy can make you want to hit back or compete with the new step-parent to show that you're better than them in some way. Commonly that means undermining the step-parent's authority with your children, 'Ignore her; she doesn't know what she's talking about,' or taking the children on more expensive holidays and buying them more expensive presents. Gabriella made a really interesting comment about this to me over lunch today, 'When Dad first got married again he and his wife started spending more on presents than you were. Steph and I thought you'd be jealous and were nervous about mentioning the presents to you. We also thought you'd want to try and compete and get us better presents than them because that's what my friend's mum did. At first I thought, great, better presents. But I was actually relieved when you didn't seem bothered. Who wants a mother, like my friend's, who is so freakily immature that she resorts to competing for her children's love like that? As if we can't see through that sort of thing and it actually makes any difference? It's just disturbing when parents act like that.'

Children will sometimes make disparaging remarks about a step-parent and it can be very tempting to laugh or go along with the bitching, particularly if you do have cause to dislike them but that will undermine what you're trying to achieve. Your children will be happiest if they are able to establish a good respectful and loving relationship with the person who now shares their father or mother's life. If you're interested in their happiness you should help them achieve that. As payback you'll then find you have someone else in the parenting 'team' that will help solve any crises in your children's lives.

Many ex-wives and ex-husbands would like to see their ex's new marriage break down and may even use the children as a weapon to bring about that outcome. But, as I've already said, a second divorce can hurt children as much, and sometimes even more, than the first one, however much you think your children want the step-parent out of their lives. Lumbering a new step-parent with children can be one way that an abandoned partner can try to get back at their ex and their new partner. One mother, who made her ex and his new wife have the children every holiday and most weekends told me; 'She stole my husband so she can look after his children.' She really didn't see what was wrong with that until I pointed out that her children were now being cared for, and raised by, someone who didn't love them, knew they were thrust on her as a 'punishment' and probably resented if not actively hated them.

### Claire's story:

I married my husband, Ian, six years ago when I was 33. I had no children but he had two boys from his previous marriage. As soon as we started to live together, his ex-wife, Sally, said that she was unable to have the children as much and told Ian that he could have them half the week and every weekend. Ian was really pleased, as he's devoted to the boys, but I could see straight away that it would stop us having much time together.

To begin with, as Ian was working, it was me who had to take on the role of main carer, sacrificing my career in the process; although we've now swapped roles. Every weekend, even when it's my birthday, we can't go anywhere together, as we have to take the boys to football and other activities. When we do go on holiday we always have to take them with us, which I really resent, as all they do is complain and make the experience miserable.

I have all the drawbacks of being a parent without any of the pleasures. I've been really shocked by how selfish children are but I'm not in a position to do anything about it like I would if they were my own children. Ian always puts his children first and I have no life at all. Sally won't ever take them more than she does now, even though I've pleaded with her to have them just one weekend a month. Ian and Sally were separated before we met but I still think she blames me for the divorce and is very happy to use me. My own parents have now had a go at Ian about the situation and my father is taking the boys away so that I can have one week where Ian and I can be a couple.

It's assumed that I should take on the duties and make the sacrifices of a mother but my role is not recognised like that. In all the time that I've effectively acted as their mother I've never had even a card from my stepsons for my birthday, Christmas or anything else. Neither Ian nor Sally think to encourage their children to recognise all I've done for them. What I've only just started to admit to myself is that I really resent the children, to the point of hatred, and I dread them coming back to us from their mother. It also now makes me question my marriage, as this is not the way I want to live.

Sometimes there will be an issue that you feel you should raise, particularly if it's something easily solved. Address it in a non-confrontational way and start from the assumption that you have only part of the story. Don't tell the children words to the effect of 'I'll sort her out!', as that tells the children that there will be a battle, which is pretty frightening. Instead simply tell them that you'll speak to the step-parent and your ex to find out what's happening then find a time when you can discuss the issue with the step-parent in a non-confrontational way. Quite often when you hear the full story your perceptions will dramatically change. Try to make the conversation face to face, particularly if it's likely to be a difficult one. Phone calls and e-mails are best avoided, because quite often the lack of non-verbal feedback will distort understanding. Put your pride and your superior 'ownership' of the child to one side and only seek to ensure the child's safety and happiness. The step-parent and your ex may genuinely not realise the impact of what they've done and be happy to address it.

### Dave's story:

My three daughters from my first marriage would come to stay every other weekend and a couple of nights during the week. They got on well with my stepdaughters and my new wife. However when the eldest girl, Rhiannon, left home to go to university we didn't see her much. I thought she was just caught up with her new life but my ex-wife phoned me one day to say that Rhiannon was really upset that we didn't seem to want to see her any more. She didn't feel she should come to our house without an invitation from us and when she didn't get one she'd go and see my ex and cry on her shoulder, thinking that she wasn't included in our lives any more. I assumed she would realise that she was always welcome.

Instead of being confrontational it's therefore far better to be supportive of your children's stepmother or stepfather. I don't want my children to feel that they have to avoid mentioning their stepmother and I want them to enjoy the time they spend with their dad, and she's now part of that. I don't agree with everything she says and does, and I'm sure she feels the same about me, of course we don't, we're two different people with different priorities on child caring and it would be amazing if we did agree on everything. Those disagreements are therefore irrelevant compared to the task of ensuring that the children that we now effectively share feel secure and comfortable in both homes and are not caught in the crossfire of us trying to score points off each other.

## Step-siblings

Don't force or expect stepchildren to get on together; just because you love each other, why should they? If they do, great, if they don't, try to accommodate that. Like when you're introducing your friends, try and find some common ground between the two sets of children (other than their disgust that two old people should be so loved-up). Make sure they each respect each other's property and don't lend out your children's stuff to your stepchildren in an attempt to get on their good side, 'I'm sure Harry won't mind you borrowing his new coat.' Harry will mind that you're more interested in pleasing your new children than worrying about 'stealing' his stuff and it won't help relations at all. Establish some codes of behaviour so that everyone feels that this is their home where they can feel safe and respected.

You can't keep things equal between stepchildren because you only manage half the equation. The children have to understand that if one of them has a less generous parent then that's not the business of the other parent and their partner. You shouldn't try to make up for it because you'll never make it 'fair' and you'll be giving the child the message that you disapprove of their other parent. In addition you're encouraging the child to play one of you off against the other. I personally know one child who deliberately deceives her mother about the presents she gets from her father so that her mother and stepfather buy her extra, to the disgust of the step-siblings (who know the truth) and are therefore the ones that feel they lose out.

It's very likely that if you both have children there will be some jealousy over how much time you spend with your own children versus your stepchildren. Gabriella spoke to me of her worries about her stepsister and her father, 'She's always with my dad except the odd weekend when she's with her dad and I used to be really jealous because he's my dad not hers and she's getting all that time with him that I'm not. Then I realised that she must feel the same as me, as her dad has children and stepchildren and she's not with him much, so we're both in the same boat.'

Jealousy can be the cause of bad behaviour that appears at first to be unrelated. Like adults, children often judge themselves against other people and, if they lack confidence, only see the ways in which they're not as good. Your child will probably judge themselves against their new step-siblings and may decide a step-sibling is 'better' than them. This step-sibling (through no one's fault) will then make your child feel inferior and less worthy of your love in the new family in which they find themselves competing for your attention. Your child will then struggle to be 'as good' as their step-sibling and, when they find they can't, hate the step-sibling and try to undermine them to make them look bad.

The best way to combat this is to make sure that your children understand their own worth. Spell it out to them that they're loved just as much as the other child and how pleased you are that they're them and not someone else. Tell them, honestly, what their attributes are while not undermining those of the child they're jealous of. Children need to understand that we're all different; they need to learn to admire and be pleased for others who do things well but just as importantly be pleased with themselves for their qualities.

## Maria's story:

Eva (who was 13 at the time) was being a complete pain; she'd moan about everything and was always fighting with her stepsister, Jane, which was difficult because they had to share a bedroom. Eventually in a conversation I was having with Eva it slipped out that she was jealous of Jane. I was really surprised as a tearful Eva told me how ugly she felt next to Jane and how she wished she could dance like Jane and how much we all must love Jane because she was never in trouble like she was.

I put my arm around Eva and agreed that Jane was very pretty and was a great dancer then told her how glad I was that she was her and not Jane. Eva looked at me really shocked; she obviously assumed that everyone shared her view that Jane was better than her. That look made me really sad for her. I wished I'd seen the problem earlier. To cover up the fact I was welling up, I hugged Eva closer and told her how proud she should be of being Eva and that she should never try to be Jane because how ever hard she tried she would never be her.

I was aware that Jane could possibly hear us (or it might be repeated) so I was careful what I said next. I wanted Eva and Jane to both realise that they both should be proud of themselves. Eva was not so good at dancing as Jane but she was much better at sport; Jane had lovely blonde hair but Eva had the most beautiful exotic eyes. Jane was much more even tempered, which made her easier to live with, but Eva was more passionate about things, which made her fun to be around. I didn't lie to Eva or even exaggerate; I just got her to appreciate what she had instead of envying what Jane had.

The effect on Eva of this conversation was like someone had waved a magic wand. She became a completely different child. Of course she still had the temper but it was a flash rather than the constant misery she had been. Her confidence and school work soared and Jane and Eva went from enemies to good friends. It still makes me feel very warm when I walk past their room and they're helping each other get ready to go out to a party.

You're probably aware that many psychologists believe that your position in your family (oldest, middle, youngest or only child) has a huge influence on who you are as a person. The oldest are believed to be the most serious and studious of the family who take on responsibility for others. Only children grow up with an advanced ability to get on with adults but with less ability to compete with others. Youngest children grow up expecting everyone to do everything for them and can be irresponsible with money. In my experience these stereotypes aren't always true but the positioning can have a strong influence on a child's understanding of their place and importance in the world. This will obviously be muddled when you merge two families of children and understanding the stereotypes can give you an insight into the emotional issues that the children might experience. For example:

- An only child may feel particularly under threat when they suddenly have to compete for time, attention and resources.
- An older child may feel 'demoted' if they're given step-siblings who are older than them.
- The child who had been the youngest may find that they can't play the 'baby' card any more, as you expect them to set an example and behave more responsibly than their new younger step-siblings.

An even bigger threat to children than having to share a home with new step-siblings is the birth of a new child in the new family. Even in 'intact' families this is a stressful time for your children. To understand how they're feeling, try to see it from their viewpoint. How would you feel if your husband or wife told you that they now had a new lover and you shouldn't be jealous because they still loved you just as much? This is how many children, in 'intact' families, feel about a new baby taking your attention and love away from them. Where that new baby doesn't have the baggage of the divorce, this feeling is intensified. Unlike your existing children, the baby is some-one you both share and love.

*Kevin's story:*

My parents separated and divorced when I was two. They both remarried and had more children. Although I don't remember the divorce I had a very unhappy childhood. I never felt I belonged in either of the two new happy families. I was the spare part that reminded both families of their unhappy pasts. I used to hide away in my room a lot because I thought they wanted me out of the way. Until very recently, I'm now 31, I always assumed my company wasn't wanted by anyone. I had no self-confidence or belief in my own worth at all, even though I was very successful at work (I put it down to luck). People used to exploit this and I was bullied a lot, both as a child and as an adult.

With young children, one of the best tricks I was told was to stage manage the children's first meeting with the new baby. When your children (and your partner's children) come to visit the mother and new child in hospital ensure that the baby is in the cot and don't mention it until they do. Instead give them all your attention. When they do ask let them find a wrapped present in the cot to each child from the new baby. You explain to the child that the present is from their new brother or sister as a thank you for sharing their mum/dad and stepmum/stepdad. The present should be something they've been really keen to have so it feels particularly special. I did this with Steph and for years (until she was about eight) if anyone asked how she got on with her sister she always told them that Gabriella had given her Mickey Mouse. Of course she eventually realised that Gabriella couldn't have got it but it meant her earliest memories were warm ones in which her 'sacrifice' was recognised. I think it would work particularly well in the case of new families formed from broken ones because it says to the existing children that the baby is joining the family, not taking precedence over the old one. One bit of advice: do make sure that the presents are small in size, particularly if you have a lot of children between you, or the poor baby will get crushed.

## Handling your ex's stepchildren

Your children might now have stepbrothers and stepsisters and half-brothers and half-sisters that are absolutely nothing to do with you; you might never even get to meet them. I've no idea about the etiquette of the situation but my guide has been to treat these children, if they do appear at my door (which they have done), like a special friend of my children's and to take account of their needs, and the need to create a loving family, when I'm trying to arrange things myself. For example, if I knew it was their birthday, I would take account of that when making my own plans to ensure that they could include my children if they wished to. There is an African saying, which I love, that says it takes a whole community to raise a child. Although society would not expect you to take any responsibility for these children, as your actions can affect their happiness, I think you have a duty to consider them. Like your children, these children have probably gone through the breakdown of their own parents' relationship so, as a concerned adult, you should not make their lives any more difficult. That sounds obvious but, from what I've seen, too many parents don't share that view: 'Why should I be bothered with *her* children; she should have thought of their happiness before she stole my husband.'

Making your children's new step-siblings and half-siblings feel welcome can also add to the sense of extended loving family that children should be surrounded by as opposed to the warring and very separate factions that many children have to grow up with. It will also mean that your children can be proud of you with these step-siblings instead of ashamed of your behaviour (which I've seen too often).

## Christmas and other social minefields

Once people get divorced and remarry, relationships become very complicated which can make many social situations and arrangements politically and practically very complex. With any family, it can be a challenging to ensure you invite the right people and don't offend anyone; with a divorced family, I think it's pretty well impossible. My ex-mother-in-law used to consider her ex-son-in-law's stepchildren by his new wife to be her grandchildren, and sometimes their step-siblings through their father's remarriage, so many of them turned up to family celebrations. Confused? I was too. Your children can have step-siblings who have step-siblings, who have step-siblings ad infinitum. It might feel like the chain of families connected like this goes on for ever and that everyone in the world is related in one big divorced family.

This tends to cause most problems at Christmas and other big celebrations. The only way to resolve it is to take turns and then try and make sure the other one gets to see his or her children as close to the celebration as possible. If you need to change things give plenty of warning, as you may find that your simple request to have the children on the 23rd rather than the 24th of December affects some woman in Outer

Mongolia connected to your children through this chain. Like with a house buying chain, there is nothing you can really do about it but the worst thing you can do is try to bully everyone into doing what you want, as that will simply ensure they feel no moral obligation to help you out in the future.

On the children's birthdays give them the chance to see both of you. If they're very young and are having a party invite your ex to be there (with his or her new partner) if you can bear it without ruining the day. As children get older, assume that they'll stay with whoever's shift they're on but invite them round to get presents, etc.

On other family celebration days offer your ex the children but don't assume they want them (unless it's their shift); they could be planning something that doesn't include them. You should make your own preferences known as early as possible if you want to be sure of including your children.

Children will want, and should be encouraged, to buy both their parents presents for birthdays, Mother's Days, etc. If they're young they'll probably not have their own money to do it and if one of you doesn't have a new partner to give them the money they'll be put in the difficult position of not being able to give their mother or father a present. To resolve this, I agreed with my ex that I gave the children £20 ($40) each to buy presents for him and he did the same for me. When the children were young we also helped in the choosing of the presents and made sure they were bought and delivered in time.

## Weddings

I'm pretty sure that many of the people who get married in Vegas or on a beach have first looked at their splintered families and shuddered at the idea of trying to get everyone together and behaving well enough to have a civilised, let alone happy, wedding. If you're lucky enough for your children to want to include you don't try and take over and force decisions on them or they'll be off to Vegas on the next plane. Instead make it very clear that it's their day and that you won't make life difficult for them by being oversensitive about who's invited and what that means. You can of course make suggestions but try not to be offended if they want you to sit next to your ex all day while your spouse of the last 15 years is left at home.

It's very common for parents to use their children's wedding as a chance to catch up on all the relatives they never see and with stepfamilies that can get very unwieldy. If you don't see these relatives often the chances are your children will hardly know them so, unless you're paying them to have a really huge affair, let them save the places for the friends that do share their lives and have been there for them over the years. And if one of those people is a step-relation that you hate, grit your teeth and put on the best act you can.

If you make it to the baptisms of your grandchildren I'm guessing you don't need any more advice from me; except to remember your experiences to help your grandchildren through their parents' divorces (and don't take sides!).

# Conclusion – Happily Ever After?

- How to make divorce a positive experience
- The joys of having single parents
- The joys of stepfamilies
- Why divorce can be good for your children
- The keys to making it work
- A last word

After all the doom and gloom I didn't want to end without telling you the good news. I almost feel I should whisper this for fear of shocking you too much but the truth is that I and many of the people I spoke to found that children can actually *gain* from their parents getting divorced.

The last six chapters have focused on how to handle divorce to avoid it causing emotional harm to children. You probably picked up on the fact that the emotional harm is not normally done by nasty scheming adults out to hurt children but by normal loving parents who simply didn't anticipate the effect of what they believed was normal, justified behaviour or failed to take the long-term view. This last chapter switches to the positive: how can your children gain from divorce and how can you ensure that your behaviour makes this happen?

## How to make divorce a positive experience

How much of what you've read in this book do you believe? What about the things you disagreed with? Would you begin to believe what I said if you saw the advice elsewhere? Most of us start to believe something if we hear it often enough; we believe that one person can and often is wrong but large numbers of people are unlikely to get it wrong; and of course that's the theory behind democracy. What do your children hear about divorce and the way it will affect them? Our media, and many adults, tell our children that they come from 'broken homes' which excuses everything from performing badly at school right the way through to criminal behaviour. I think it can be a self-fulfilling prophecy; if children hear that often enough they'll believe it and live up to these low expectations. If you expect and are too ready to forgive people for behaving badly they usually do.

When you talk to people you realise that almost everyone has been through some terrible experiences. You only become a long-term victim of those experiences if you choose to and, as a parent, you shouldn't encourage your children to choose to be the victim. To have the highs in life you have to have the lows. My daughters saw my ex and I happy as a couple and enjoying our relationship; they saw us deeply hurt and they see us happy again. You can teach your children to be like the Dickens' character, Miss Havisham, and wallow for ever in self-pity or you can support them through the bad times and show them that life can be great again.

I saw an article in the paper today about a man who'd lost his wife and three daughters in the tsunami of 2004. It's difficult for most of us to even begin to understand how that must have felt. He was in the paper because his new wife had just given birth to triplets, all girls. If you think your life, and that of your children, is destroyed and will never be the same again because of your ex-partner, think of that man. I would not have blamed him if he'd spent the rest of his life in mourning, but he chose not to. He moved on and has found happiness again. I'm sure he does still mourn his lost family but he's recognised that it won't bring them back and that it would make him another victim if he didn't find a way to move on.

As I hope you realise, from the rest of this book, I work very hard to make things as good as they can be for my children but I don't believe in reinforcing the idea that they're hard done by or letting them get dramatic about their 'suffering'. One mother I spoke to, who had young children at the time of her divorce, took a particularly proactive stand on this one and regularly pointed out successful people on TV whose parents had been divorced. She did this to reinforce in her children's minds the idea that having divorced parents is no excuse not to do well in life. I can't help wondering how fed up her children are going to get with so many interruptions but it might go some way to counteract the social pressure that reinforces the idea that they're bound to fail.

Many parents and other adults will 'help' children going through the break-up of their parents' marriage by sympathising with how awful things are or will be. In effect they're instructing their children to be miserable. They will take their children to counsellors before the children have even expressed any upset or emphasise how terribly the other parent has behaved towards them, instead of letting children come to their own conclusions, which they will. Children will lap up the attention their 'misery' is giving them and know that the best way of keeping that attention is to go along with the idea that they're suffering, which will not be difficult because they'll soon believe it themselves. In effect some children are talked into being upset by concerned adults. Usually this is done out of a genuine desire to help although I expect sometimes the children's grief is a useful stick with which to beat an errant ex to try to make him/her feel even more guilty. To avoid this, be careful of the sympathy you give, as it can focus your children's minds on the negative rather than the positive and can stop them moving on and finding the good in life again. There were two incidents in my life recently that demonstrated this:

- I lost a lot of weight, over a stone (14 pounds), and was nearly at my ideal weight. I was really happy about that until a friend 'sympathised' with me for how frustrated I must be at the weight coming off so slowly and how it must be annoying that after three months I still couldn't get into size tens in every shop. I started to immediately focus on my failure and the problems I was still experiencing rather than being motivated by my success so far. It made me want to end the diet and go back to overeating. My friend's 'sympathy' had turned my satisfaction into something to be depressed about.

- My cat had to have a hysterectomy. I was expecting her to lie in her basket for days staring mournfully into space feeling sorry for herself and waiting for us to give her lots of attention and affection. I know that's how I'd behave. Instead, once the anaesthetic had worn off, she was trying to get on with life in pretty much the same way she usually did. She was a bit groggy, a bit confused, but she certainly wasn't upset or feeling sorry for herself. Why? Because no one had told her she should be sitting around lapping up sympathy. She was able to get up so that's what she did.

So while addressing and being sympathetic to all their worries, listen hard for what they actually are and don't make the mistake of putting depressing thoughts and ideas into your children's heads. You should also think hard, from your children's viewpoint, what might be positive about the divorce, and encourage them to think that way. Rather than, 'Poor you, I know how terrible this will be for you.' Try, 'You'll get a break from each of your parents, you'll have two bedrooms, two lots of parents to give you presents and take you on holiday and a new sister to hang round with when the other gets irritating.' Instead of saying, 'How awful that you won't see your dad much' you should say, 'I bet you're pleased that you're now going to get time with your dad when he's not busy with other stuff' and then make sure that happens. Instead of saying, 'How awful that you've got to move,' ask them how they want their new bedroom decorated.

The effect of being positive can have a truly dramatic effect on children. One child, whose parents were convinced that their daughter must be suffering much more than she was letting on but had deliberately focused on the positive, told her counsellor, 'It was really cool when they got a divorce. I got two holidays, two lots of Christmas presents, two lots of birthday presents and no more shouting!'

Some marriages end very badly and with terrible bitterness, but even there, if you look for it, over time you can see the positives. It really is up to you to build from them rather that let them pull you down.

## Molly's story:

I married young and had never worked or gained any qualifications. My husband had a very good job so I didn't worry about it. However he suddenly left me for another woman when our two sons were still babies and didn't give me any money. We had to go from a comfortable detached house to emergency public housing. I struggled to afford food while he continued to live in style with his mistress who he eventually married (and in time, having fathered two more children, left for yet another woman).

It was a terrible time but I don't regret any of it. I now own my own home and am happily married. My sons grew up with huge ambition to better themselves and both are very successful. It would have been easy to stay bitter but if I hadn't married the man I did I wouldn't have my sons: if he'd not left when he did I would have stayed married to a man who clearly had no morals and I would not have found the happiness I have. If we'd not struggled like we did I doubt my sons would have had so much drive to succeed. My ex-husband is now alone and my sons have very little to do with him. Although for years I was angry at the unfairness of it, in time, people get the life they deserve.

## The joys of having single parents

My daughters and I didn't settle into our new routine straight away; there were difficult times. I don't have time to be the image of the perfect mother that so many of us guilt-ridden parents hold in our heads, but can never be. I'm sure you know the image I'm referring to; the one of the gingham-aproned mother baking cakes, ready and waiting to attend to her children's every need? The problem is that image is from the 1950s. Like most parents today, particularly single parents, I have to hold down a job which sometimes creates the most impossible conflict in priorities; do I let down my colleagues at a critical stage in a project or do I attend 'Clever Cat's Tea Party', which is just as critical to my daughter being able to show me her achievements? How bad is my daughter's cold; is it bad enough to miss a critical meeting to care for her or will she be fine at the childminder's? Worst of all was when my daughter, then three years old, forgot to put her knickers on. Of course I'd dressed her but she had taken them off again and only told me this bit of news halfway to nursery when turning back meant being very late for a meeting I was due to chair at the Cabinet Office. I had a grim choice, my daughter arriving knickerless at nursery or walking in late in front of all those disapproving suits and lying about why I was late (well, would you have told the truth?). I therefore fully appreciate how much of a struggle it can be but even that can be positive.

Children of single parents have to be more self-sufficient. My children have told me themselves that they're better prepared for life than their friends whose mothers still do everything for them. Stephanie cooked me a full roast dinner last week when many girls of her age can't even boil an egg.

My daughters can see that life is not all about men or being a mother. They know that education is important because ultimately they're responsible for their economic and emotional welfare. It's not just about finding a man and being happy ever after; there are lots of other things that are important in life but family should always be there for each other; even if that sometimes requires lots of effort, it's worth it.

### Siobhan's story:

There have been some really tough times; I even had to take three months off work with depression once, but life is much better now than it would have been, for all of us. Two things really made the difference: my ex and I continuing to support each other in parenting (if you have that you're not a single parent with all those stresses) and making sure that the children always felt loved, by both of us so we backed each other up on that one too. We both made bad, insensitive decisions sometimes, we're human, but rather than use that to get one up on each other with the children we always stressed what a great parent the other one was and how much they loved them.

There are many advantages to getting divorced that no one ever talks about. It's always seen as a disaster for children; we're the cause of all the social problems in the world, aren't we? The experts in the books tell us our children never recover from the divorce. If it didn't embarrass them I'd exhibit my children as exhibits; happy well-adjusted young adults that enjoyed their childhoods with both their parents who happened to live in different houses. No big deal! No excuse for bad behaviour or emotional problems.

Parents who have had to completely rethink their role in the family because of a divorce often re-think other parts of their lives too. Instead of carrying along in the same old rut they often look around them and reassess things. This can be unsettling for the children who are along for the ride whether they want it or not but it can also make their lives richer. As always, it depends how you handle it and whether you remember in all the excitement to provide the structure, care and support your children still need.

As a direct result of my divorce, my children have met a huge variety of new people beyond the circle of married couples I used to spend most of my time with. They love these exciting, younger single people, as they're more relevant role models than their friends' mothers. My daughter, at just 19, is thinking of setting up her own business. Would she have thought this was possible if she hadn't met a friend of mine who set up a successful business at her age?

In an 'intact' happy family the parents are often not seen as real people by the children; they're 'parents' who don't really have a life beyond that role in the eyes of their children until something happens to change that. I've even seen that attitude in 'children' in their 30s and it was highlighted by the disproportionate distress I found that adult children felt towards their parents getting divorced compared to those that experienced it as children.

I genuinely feel closer to my daughters. Most children crave one-to-one time but in a good marriage the children can feel like gooseberries on their parents' relationship. Eleanor, who has two small sons and divorced two years ago, agrees, 'I was devastated when my ex-husband left but I can now see some positives. I know that I have a bond with my sons that I wouldn't have had if I'd still been married. I also find that people are friendlier to me now. Before I think they thought my life was too perfect and now I'm part of their world. There is a natural bond between people who've been divorced and I'm enjoying life now. It took me 18 months to stop pining for my ex-husband but now I'm really getting on with my life.'

Many men I've spoken to had little to do with their children, before the divorce. It was only the fear of losing their children and then being given clear blocks of time with them that made them realise what they'd been missing by not getting more involved. Where the mother acts fairly, fathers can come out of a divorce with a much closer relationship to their children than they had before it.

Mark, whose wife left him with four young children, also agrees, 'The children and I all had to pull closer to make things work. They could see I was struggling to begin with; I didn't hide it, so the older ones helped, I showed my appreciation and they grew in confidence. We became a team, with everyone doing their bit to make our lives work. We're much closer because of it.'

As I stressed earlier, I'm very clear with them that I'm their mother, not their friend; I'm there to be an emotional crutch for them, not the other way round. But with one less adult in the family we share the ups and downs of life more, as well as the exciting news and developments in life. I think it's because normally there is a bit of 'them' and 'us' (children and parents) about family life, whereas in a one-parent family it is all about the individuals.

My own daughter, Gabriella, told me, 'I'm much closer to you than most of my mates are to their mums. You understand my life better and you treat me more like an adult, because there aren't any other adults in the house. I actually prefer it.' Which means that Gabriella has now gone from thinking, 'It's no big deal really' to concluding that she's had lots of advantages which make up for the packing which she still hates.

### Richard's story:

My parents got divorced when I was about ten. I still feel sick when I think about that time. I was really scared about what was going to happen to us. I used to sit on the stairs and listen to my parents arguing and discussing stuff to try and find out what would happen.

I was really angry with them to begin with but then I realised how stupid that was; I wasn't the only one in that situation; in fact at school it made you part of a pretty cool group. Once I stopped feeling sorry for myself things were OK. My dad used to make a special effort to see us, whereas before the divorce he hardly seemed to notice us. Mum was much happier and that made the house feel a more relaxed place.

Dad got a new girlfriend pretty quickly and she wasn't used to children so she'd try all sorts of things to get us to like her. They were all over each other for a while and that was a bit embarrassing, particularly if I had mates back, but it was far better than the arguments we used to have to listen to. It also meant that when dad started talking to me about women I knew he had recent knowledge of what it was like to date so we became more like mates. I think that was the best thing about the divorce; I'm much closer to my dad than I would have been; I'm sure of that.

## Single parents and young children

You don't need me to tell you that young children demand a lot of your time. When you're married you can easily get buried under those demands and be 'just' a mother. If you share care after your divorce you should find you have time to yourself again. That sounds callous and uncaring to your children but the break will give you a chance to 'recharge' and you'll probably be less stressful with them than when you've got them full time. Use the free time to see people or attend events that you know they'd hate getting dragged along to.

I never liked relying on babysitters; they make going out much more difficult and expensive, you normally spend the evening worrying about getting home on time and you're rarely completely confident that they're reliable. The only exception is if you have a relative who's happy to help out, but even then you can feel guilty about using them too much. An amicable divorce, where your ex lives close, should mean that you never need babysitters again. You can obviously use the time when your children are at their dad or mum's place to go out, hassle-free, and if you help your ex out when he or she needs someone, he or she will probably return the favour. Your ex is usually the best babysitter you could find as they're the one person who loves and cares about them as much as you do so you can go out confident that you're not putting your children at risk, and that they won't be at all unsettled by the experience.

Younger children are likely to adapt quickly to the new circumstances; things that seem odd and difficult to you will soon be seen as a normal part of life and they may even be shocked that everyone doesn't have time separately with Mum and Dad.

## Single parents and teenagers

One of the biggest challenges most parents face is the teenage years and the perception of most teenagers that parents have no idea what they're up against so dismiss all advice and attempt at helping. This can lead to a really stressful period which can go on for months (if you're really lucky) or more usually years when nothing you do or say is taken in the loving way you meant it. Children often reach their 20s before they realise that they really should have listened to their parents' advice.

By contrast one of the most unexpected positive side effects of my divorce is that my children give me the impression that they accept that I know what I'm talking about, particularly when my advice relates to a judgement on them dating someone. They actually listen to what I say and act on it (or are very good at pretending they do). As another teenager explained to me, 'Parents who've stayed married haven't dated since the dark ages (I think she meant nearly 20 years) by the time our generation starts to date. What do they know?' As a married mother, I think I would have questioned that and argued that I've been there and do remember what it's like. But, as a divorcee soon discovers, the world has moved on so much that much of what they remember is probably not relevant and teenagers can easily spot that lack of real understanding.

It's very easy to forget the horrors and joys of dating again, but I'm there with them now. I know that telling someone that 'there are more fish in the sea' when they're grieving the loss and rejection of someone they love is at best insensitive. I know how manipulative men (and women, I'm sure) can really be and how overwhelming and difficult it is to control the first rush of excitement at finding someone you really click with. I know how easy it is to find yourself stuck after a party with no means home other than a dodgy taxi and that it's far more useful to give them an uncomplaining lift at 3 am than criticise them for it and risk them taking a less safe option next time. As a single woman, I know better than my married friends about the pressures out there today and how prevalent things such as drugs are. In short I think I'm in a much better position to anticipate both the dangers and the emotional roller coaster they're on. It makes it easier for me to judge when to step in and when it's better to leave them to find out for themselves. They know that, 'How are you getting home?' is not an accusation that they're not capable of looking after themselves; it's an offer of help in a tricky situation.

Some people are very good at hiding their true selves behind a sea of charm and sex appeal. Children are remarkably good at exposing that. I certainly never listened to my parents and I don't actually remember them risking a judgement on my dates but I do trust my daughters' judgement on the men and friends I bring home. They know me better than almost anyone, like I do them, so if they don't trust or like a man or friend I listen and they've always been right. That teaches them that those that love them will look out for them out of love and not out of a desire to interfere. They return that respect and listen to me when I make a similar judgement. They've learned what to look for in people; we've all sat and discussed the signs of 'controllers' and 'players'. We're all going through the experience together. We know that 'love is blind' which means that someone's faults are more likely to be recognised by someone who isn't attracted to them. Like with all other knowledge in life, we're most likely to listen to someone who we believe knows what they're talking about and people married for decades have lost their dating currency in the eyes of a teenager.

We still fall out sometimes, but not any more frequently than any other strong-minded mother and teenage daughters. It's normal; it would be weird if we didn't and certainly isn't anything to do with the divorce. But those times do make me realise that I actually have it much easier than my still-married friends. My daughters and I get 'time out' from each other and when we're really fed up it gives us all a chance to put things into perspective and realise how much we really value each other; being apart is definitely good for our relationship. To put it into Gabriella's words, 'I prefer it, when I get sick of one of you it's about the time I get to move house.' Meanwhile I get to have regular holidays from teenage angst and can be a single woman with the freedom of coming and going without worrying about who is picking up whom, and when and whether they've actually eaten anything hot or even vaguely healthy.

Packing every few weeks to move from one house to another is never ideal. My daughter still complains about it; but she does insist on taking everything and even that has an unexpected benefit. Teenagers are legendary for the untidiness of their rooms. One of mine is particularly bad but every couple of weeks she goes to her dad's and takes most of her things with her. I can then blitz a nearly empty room which limits how bad it can really get and satisfies me that it doesn't have time to become a health hazard. Without that blitz, I think the rats would be squatting there and I'd have no crockery. I recognise that, depending on your attitude to these things, this will either be a minor benefit and you'll question why I even mention it or a reason to get divorced even if you're happily married. I'm afraid it makes me a very happy woman to have that room clean and tidy for at least some of the time. More importantly, it's one less stress point for my daughter and I to fall out over.

## The joys of stepfamilies

Much of the above doesn't apply if you form a new relationship straight away and a stepfamily emerges. These too have their advantages. After all the warnings and the fairy tales of wicked step-parents these relationships can work well. I know many adults who regard their stepmothers and stepfathers just as highly and with as much affection as their own parents. It didn't happen straight away, or without work on both sides, but once you overcome the jealousy and competition the shared bond of loving someone and wanting their happiness can be a powerful driver to bring the people around them together.

Traditional families can be very closed institutions with one set of values and views on the world. With stepfamilies, children will be exposed to different sets of values and have to learn how to live with them. If you deal with things amicably between the two households the children discover that things can be done totally differently and that neither is wrong, just different. I think that's a really important lesson in life that many adults have failed to understand and is the cause of a lot of anti-social behaviour. Finding out how to be part of a whole new family and accepting and adjusting to different values are also useful lessons for the future, particularly when children form long-term relationships and get accepted into new families as the 'in-law'.

Many stepfamilies now introduce different religions and ethnic groups to children who may previously have had fixed, and inaccurate, views about. Living with people from entirely different backgrounds in a warm family unit is an incredibly effective way of overcoming prejudices.

Your children will gain new family members, not just step-siblings and parents but new aunties, uncles and grandparents. Many of these adults will accept new children into the family very warmly, often treating them just like they would blood relatives. My own children had lost three of their grandparents by the time we divorced but with their father's remarriage they gained a new complete set and, by their accounts, their new grandparents have an uncanny resemblance to the previous ones (even sharing first names and unusual professions).

Without wishing to sound too morbid, with my ex and their stepmother, my children have a 'spare set' of parents. If I die tomorrow, economically they don't suffer at all, they just live full-time with their dad and stepmum.

I warned you to be aware of how the new stepfamily can alter the dynamics of the family by changing a child's position within it. However there are positive aspects to this too.

Many children will have dreamed of having younger or older siblings – or just someone else, if an only child. With the step-family, those dreams are realised. A youngest child may find herself older than her new siblings with the wonderful power and chance to boss around that she's always dreamed of. Alternatively an older child, weary of the responsibility that brings, may have new older siblings to rely on and cadge for lifts and other favours. And of course many stepfamilies introduce the different genders as siblings for the first time. Both will benefit from the additional understanding this will give them of the opposite sex, and usually these new siblings are only part-time so don't come with as much pressure as a full-time sibling. They also introduce a whole new circle of friends and possible future dates.

Children with only one or even no siblings to argue with suddenly have a whole new 'all you can eat buffet' of family to take their bad temper out on in the comfortable knowledge that this is safe because these people are family so will still be there when they're ready to be nice again.

My daughter will happily talk of her sister's sister (by which she means her stepsister's stepsister) but I can see people with less experience of the complications of stepfamilies looking confused as to why she's not simply referred to the girl as her sister but it shows me she's accepted these girls as part of her extended family. Children can find they suddenly have someone with more street cred in their family and can latch on to the 'cool' factor. My daughter, who has always been keen on Beyoncé-style dancing, was delighted to have a new half-black sister to teach her the Harlem Shake (that bottom wiggling thing they do in R&B videos). In turn she tried to teach my 81-year-old mother: so everyone benefited!

Children love to feel that they're special to other people and they soon realise that 'family' is and should be special and, with good stepfamilies, you get more of it.

# Why divorce can be good for your children

There are people who think that the number one priority for children is for them to enjoy their childhood. This means that they believe that children should be excused from chores and be protected from all of life's harsh realities. The other view is that childhood is primarily a chance to learn about life and how to be a civilised and capable human being. That means gradually being exposed to life and its realities and being taught how to be self-sufficient as early as possible. Given the choice between having a happy childhood with no responsibilities and a childhood that prepared me well for life I would choose the latter. Life is tough and competitive; to succeed our children need to be given all the skills and experience they can get before they're judged harshly for not having them. Of course I want my children to be happy, but not at the expense of having a miserable adulthood.

A friend of mine was describing someone to me once and I picked up that they weren't that keen on the individual concerned. I pressed my friend because there was nothing bad in the description, and eventually my friend sighed and said, 'They suffer from having too content a childhood.' I instantly knew what she meant but it was not something I'd heard articulated before and I've thought about the remark a lot since. Nearly all my friends had childhoods that were disturbed in some way, my closest alarmingly so, but they're all successful individuals whose company I value often above those who've had an easier time in life. I clearly prefer the company of people who've had difficult times. The question I've been asking myself is why?

Few of us lead entirely stress-free lives; most of us have been through some truly traumatic times but we learn valuable lessons from those experiences, most importantly about people and keeping things in perspective. Children who've experienced the trauma of divorce have experienced people with raw emotions. They've seen their parents distressed and irritated and learn to pick up the emotional signals quickly, such as when to keep out the way; it's part of their survival. My experience is that this often makes them more sensitive to the feelings of others, makes them tougher individuals and gives them a more balanced, less melodramatic perspective on life.

This adds up to a startling conclusion. If both parents handle divorce, as suggested in this book, then contrary to what people commonly believe my conclusion is that children can be made warmer individuals who are closer to their parents as a direct result of it. Of course that's not saying that trauma is a good thing for children; just that too much protection from the harsh realities of life can make children less sensitive than their friends who've come face to face with it and learned how to survive. If you've fought a battle and won then you're not so frightened of the next one. But if the battle has been bad and bloody, as is so commonly the case with divorce (just look at the celebrity battles raging now), then of course the end result is children without the foundations and structures to give them the confidence to go out in the world, form close loving relationships and take the risks they need to. So, as I said at the beginning, it's not divorce that's bad for children it's the adversarial way that society continues to handle it.

### Craig's story:

When my wife said she wanted a divorce I was devastated. I believed our marriage would last for ever. We had two small boys and, from what all my mates had told me, I thought I'd have to fight to be part of their lives.

However 15 years on I now believe that the divorce was the best thing that could have happened, for all of us. I'm married again and much happier than I ever was with my ex; she wasn't a bad person but we irritated each other all the time so there were constant fights. I thought that was how married life was but I now know that it shouldn't be like that; my new marriage is calm and we enjoy every moment we spend together.

My ex has always been fair with the boys; they've spent lots of time with me and she's made sure I was involved as an equal parent. We had a few rough patches, particularly when they were teenagers but that's normal, and my ex, my new wife and I handled it together. The boys are adults now and they're both happy, well-adjusted kids that I couldn't be more proud of. I don't think they would be the people they are if they'd grown up with my ex and me fighting all the time.

## The keys to making it work

1. Recognise the moral rights of your children to both their parents over and above any of your rights.

2. Draw up your own separation agreement before you go to a lawyer and see a mediator (not a lawyer) if you get into problems over it.

3. Organise the divorce so that both of you can continue to be full-time parents.

4. Live as close as you can to each other.

5. Keep the communications channels open between you.

6. Forget that you were a couple; your only relationship now is as a united parenting team.

7. Keep things amicable but don't be afraid of letting the children know that you are upset.

8. Make as much time for your children as you can and make sure they feel loved.

9. Treat everyone (your ex, your ex's new partner and any relatives) with consideration and respect, however much you hate them. Remember that your children almost certainly love your ex and feel a strong sense of loyalty to him or her.

10. Encourage your children to enjoy the time they spend with your ex.

11. Don't try and compete with your ex.

12. Recognise what's important to your children's lives and don't undervalue their need for friends and out-of-school activities.

13. Plan for the future and don't assume that new people will not enter your lives.

14. Don't expect your children to feel any sense of attachment to new people important in your life, but if attachments do form, treat them with the same respect as their blood relatives.

# A last word

Having read so much about divorce six years ago and more recently for this book, when my children are young adults, I wanted to get it from the 'horse's' mouth. I was scared that I was kidding myself and there were lots of problems to come out. What were the upsets, the things we did wrong; how has it really affected them? You might have noticed that my older daughter, Stephanie, now 19, is quoted far less than her sister in this book. As Gabriella supplied me with the title, and a fair chunk of the content, I wanted the last word to be from Stephanie. She's a thoughtful, loving, sensitive soul with a very strong sense of justice who isn't at all afraid to say if things are wrong. As a tiny baby, she shocked me when one of her tiny hands patted my back in a comforting motherly fashion. When she was at primary school other parents phoned me up to thank me for raising a child that had stopped theirs from getting bullied. At secondary school she was one of the only students who never once got a detention and she sailed through her exams without me having to tell her to go and study. I therefore didn't think she had major problems but she helped me so little with this book that I was concerned there was something that she didn't want to tell me. Eventually after getting nowhere in everyday conversation I took her out to dinner and asked her the question. She looked at me confused, 'I don't know really, I never think about it. It happens to everyone. I don't think it's affected me at all.' Thanks, Steph; not a lot of material for my book there but perhaps it sums up how it should be.

# About the Author

Anne Cantelo spent her early career in the Department of Trade and Industry and the Cabinet Office. She moved to the private sector in 2000 and has since worked on projects designed to help children. Anne started CC4G (www.cc4g.net), a not for profit award-winning programme that has changed the attitude of girls to IT. More recently she set up Fit Future Ltd (www.fitfuture.co.uk/partners), a web-based teen health initiative that has been actively supported by schools, experts and celebrities.

Anne married in 1985 and separated and divorced in 2001. At the time, her two daughters were aged ten and 13 years old. She didn't spend a penny on a divorce lawyer and the title of the book is a direct quote from her younger daughter, Gabriella, about her parents' divorce to a friend.

# I Want to See My Kids!

## A Guide for Dads Who Want Contact With Their Children After Separation

### Tina Rayburn and Timothy Forder

Barely a week goes by without a news story about a father who wants to see his children but has been denied this right by the British courts. Many accounts concern more militant dads, who have been driven to express their frustration by performing some kind of daring escapade. But behind these stunts lie harsh realities – of fathers fighting to stay in their children's lives after divorce or separation and finding no support from our skewed legal system.

Having researched the field, Tina Rayburn and Timothy Forder were overwhelmed by the evidence of so many families being destroyed by the family court system. They found scores of cases where children's wishes were overlooked and fathers were left powerless to fight back. In most basic terms, they discovered that once the arena of the family court system has been entered, anything resembling family life was over for Dad.

*I Want to See My Kids!* gives real-life examples of the terrible way families are ripped apart after divorce. As well as this, it exposes all the issues dads face when going through separation or divorce, including advice on choosing legal representation, what role the courts have, what contact means, what happens when things break down, and the impact on children and the extended family. With a helpful resources section to gain further information and support, this book is an indispensable guide to help dads stay part of their children's lives.

Non-fiction: Parenting/Current Affairs
1-904132-59-6
£10.99
www.fusionpress.co.uk